What Is the Purpose of This Teacher Guide?

The purpose of this Teacher Guide is to provide teachers and other classroom support staff with step-by-step instructions and the necessary background information to effectively implement the *Olweus Bullying Prevention Program*™ in a classroom setting.

It is important that you read through the Teacher Guide in its entirety before beginning implementation.

Throughout this guide, you will see:

RESEARCH FACTS

These facts highlight some of the important research findings that Dr. Dan Olweus, his collaborators, and other researchers have learned over more than thirty-five years of studying bullying.

IMPLEMENTATION TIPS

These tips and strategies, gleaned from others' experiences, will make program implementation easier for you.

• • •

How to Use the DVD and the CD-ROM

This Teacher Guide comes with a DVD and a CD-ROM. Here's how to use these components.

Accessing the DVD Video Resources

The DVD includes six bullying scenarios (two for grades 1–3, two for grades 4–6, and two for grades 7–8) that are to be used in a variety of ways as outlined later in this guide.

Whenever you see this icon in this guide, you are encouraged to view the DVD. To access the scenarios, put the disk in a DVD player. A menu will automatically appear on your screen. Select the scenario title, and push Play. You can pause the scenario at any time while it is playing.

Accessing the CD-ROM Print Resources

The CD-ROM contains print resources such as the handouts and templates mentioned in this guide. All of these resources are in PDF format and can be accessed using Adobe Reader. If you do not have Adobe Reader, you can download it for free at www.adobe.com.

Whenever you see this icon in this guide, there is a copy of this resource on the CD-ROM. The number on the icon corresponds to the number of the document on the CD-ROM. An SP symbol (SP) near the icon indicates the document is also available in Spanish.

To access the documents on the CD-ROM, put the disk in your computer's CD-ROM player. Open your version of Adobe Reader, and then open the documents by finding them on your CD-ROM drive. These resources cannot be modified, but they can be printed for individual classroom use without concern for copyright infringement. For a list of what is contained on the CD-ROM, see the Read Me First document on the CD-ROM.

· · ·

TEACHER GUIDE

Dan Olweus, Ph.D., and Susan P. Limber, Ph.D.

With

Vicki Crocker Flerx, Ph.D.

Nancy Mullin, M.Ed.

Jane Riese, L.S.W.

Marlene Snyder, Ph.D.

HAZELDEN

Hazelden
Center City, MN 55012-0176

1-800-328-9000
1-651-213-4590 (Fax)
www.hazelden.org

ISBN: 978-1-59285-375-5

Cover design by David Spohn
Cover photo by Tad Saddoris
Interior design and typesetting by Kinne Design

Endorsements for the *Olweus Bullying Prevention Program*

"Dr. Dan Olweus and his team have gone from strength to strength in their bullying prevention efforts with this new guide. I concur with the authors' stress on systems change as the key to violence prevention, and in expanding the audience outside the doors of the school to members of the community. Beautifully written and carefully researched, this guide comes highly recommended."

John H. Hoover
Interim Associate Dean, College of Education
St. Cloud State University, St. Cloud, Minnesota
author of *The Bullying Prevention Handbook*

"The *Olweus Bullying Prevention Program* has had a positive impact on our entire school of over 650 students and staff. We have become a safe, predictable environment for all, and all feel empowered to make a difference. Following our first full year of implementation, the reported bullying referrals have decreased by 68 percent."

Rebecca Dahl, Principal
and Casey Bertram, Assistant Principal
Edgerton Elementary School, Kalispell, Montana

"Philadelphia is the seventh largest school district in the United States. Since 2001, the *Olweus Bullying Prevention Program* has been implemented in 40 schools and our data shows that when implemented with fidelity, the program not only reduces bullying behaviors, but it effectively provides the framework for systemic improvement in school climate and safety."

Vernard Trent
Director of the Office of School Climate and Safety
School District of Philadelphia, Pennsylvania

Contents

Acknowledgments

Because the *Olweus Bullying Prevention Program* has had a long history (over thirty-five years) and has been implemented by so many around the world, it is impossible to properly acknowledge all who have contributed to its development and success. However, we want to highlight a few who have played particularly critical roles.

First, we wish to thank the many educators, students, parents, and community members who have helped to implement the program in schools worldwide and from whom we have learned so much.

We also wish to thank the many certified Olweus trainers, who, on a daily basis, work hard to help schools be successful in their implementation of the program and who seem to have a never-ending supply of energy and new ideas.

Thanks to Del Elliott and Sharon Mihalic with the Center for the Study and Prevention of Violence at the University of Colorado at Boulder for being early supporters of the program in the United States and for helping to get the word out about the *Olweus Bullying Prevention Program* through the Blueprints project.

We wish to thank the Office of Juvenile Justice and Delinquency Prevention (OJJDP) for funding the first implementation and evaluation of the program in the United States.

We wish to also acknowledge the work of those South Carolina schools that participated in the original implementation of the program in the United States.

Thanks also to those involved in the early statewide efforts in Massachusetts and Pennsylvania. Their experiences resulted in the development of many practical tools for schools, some of which are included in this guide.

Special thanks to Celia Arriaga, of the Seattle Public Schools, for her dedication in developing the Spanish translations.

We appreciate and acknowledge our many friends and colleagues at Hazelden, particularly Kris Van Hoof-Haines and Sue Thomas, who are our valued collaborators. We also thank Bonnie Dudovitz, who helped develop this guide.

And finally, we wish to thank the many schools that have submitted samples of implementation strategies for this Teacher Guide.

Introduction

Welcome to the *Olweus Bullying Prevention Program,* or *OBPP* for short. *OBPP* is the most researched and best-known bullying prevention program available today. Developed by Dr. Dan Olweus of Norway, one of the authors of this guide, *OBPP* has over thirty-five years of research behind it and has been implemented throughout the world, in countries such as the United States, Canada, England, Mexico, Iceland, Germany, Sweden, and Croatia, in addition to Norway.

OBPP is recognized by the Center for the Study and Prevention of Violence as one of only eleven (at the time of publication) Blueprints Model Programs and by the Substance Abuse and Mental Health Services Administration (SAMHSA) as a Model Program—two of the highest honors a prevention program can attain. It has also received numerous awards from other organizations dedicated to addressing the issue of bullying and violence among students.

> Olweus is pronounced
> Ol-VAY-us.

As a teacher, you know that even with your best efforts, a student may still experience bullying in classrooms, school hallways, the lunchroom, and the playground or athletic fields. And bullying isn't limited to the school grounds; it exists at school bus stops, community parks, summer camps, neighborhoods, homes, cyberspace, and anywhere that young people gather.

To stop bullying, it needs to be addressed at all levels of a student's experience. Unlike a curriculum that only addresses bullying at the classroom level and for a limited period of time, *OBPP* addresses bullying at the schoolwide, classroom, individual, and community levels.

Accordingly, students receive a consistent, reinforced message about bullying over an extended period of time and in a variety of settings. Because bullying has such wide-ranging effects, *OBPP* is designed for all students, not just those who are bullied or those who bully others.

The goal of *OBPP* is to change the norms around bullying behavior and to restructure the school setting itself so that bullying is less likely to occur or be rewarded. The implementation of *OBPP* needs to be seen as a long-term effort—not something that is "completed" in a year.

Also, because of its comprehensive approach, *OBPP* should be implemented across all grade levels in a school building at approximately the same time. Although *OBPP* takes a concerted and coordinated effort to implement, it has been proven in a number of scientific evaluations to reduce the occurrence of bullying problems and improve the school environment.

What Is Bullying?

Bullying will be defined and described in detail in chapter 2; for now, here is a general definition:

> Bullying is when someone repeatedly and on purpose
> says or does mean or hurtful things to another person
> who has a hard time defending himself or herself.

Bullying can take many forms, such as physical hitting, verbal harassment, spreading of false rumors, intentional social exclusion, and sending nasty messages on cell phones or over the Internet.

Why Is It Important to Address Bullying in Schools?

Here are some stories about bullying.

MICHAEL'S STORY

Michael, age ten, was bullied at school nearly every day. Boys punched and kicked him on the playground (just out of sight from the teachers), stole his lunch money, and called him nasty names. Michael complained to his parents and the school nurse about stomach pains and headaches and often stayed home from school, but for months he said nothing about the bullying.

As a staff we can do lots of things that will make a difference, but we are kidding ourselves if we think we're going to build positive student belonging without addressing our school's peer culture and how kids treat one another. The *Olweus Bullying Prevention Program* has helped to make positive student belonging a real possibility.

— A MIDDLE SCHOOL PRINCIPAL

When Michael's schoolwork began to suffer, his teacher asked for a meeting with Michael and his parents. At the meeting, they pressed him about why he was having trouble in school, and he finally admitted that he was being "picked on" by a few boys in his class. When asked why he hadn't told anyone sooner, he responded, "It wouldn't have done any good. I guess this is just how fourth grade is going to be."

KATIE'S STORY

Katie, an eighth-grade student with cerebral palsy, was repeatedly bullied by a male classmate. The boy called her names, such as "retard" and "stupid," blocked her path down the hall, and even rammed her wheelchair into walls. After three years of abuse, Katie and her parents successfully sued the school district. A lawsuit against the boy's family was settled out of court.

JENNY'S STORY

Jenny, a new kindergarten student, had been looking forward to riding the school bus all summer, so her mother was puzzled when, after only a week, Jenny asked if her mom could drop her off at school instead. When her mother asked why she didn't want to ride the bus anymore, Jenny admitted that some of the third- and fourth-grade girls on the bus had been taking her lunch each morning and calling her "baby."

For Students and Their Futures

Every day, there are many students, like these, who come to school terrified that they will be bullied yet again. Students who are bullied may become depressed and develop low self-esteem. Many of them develop health problems such as stomachaches and headaches, and their schoolwork is likely to suffer. Some bullied students may have suicidal thoughts and may even end their own lives. The effects on students who are bullied can last far into the future, long after they are out of school. It is an obvious human right for every student to feel safe in school and to be spared the repeated degradation and humiliation that come from being bullied.

Students who bully others also have problems but typically of a very different nature. Many bullying students engage in other "antisocial" behaviors such as breaking rules, shoplifting and vandalizing property, drinking alcohol and smoking at relatively young ages, and carrying a weapon. There are also clear indications that bullying students, in particular boys, are at a greater risk of continuing on

Duplicating this page is illegal. Do not duplicate without publisher's written permission.

xiii

an antisocial path involving crime and substance abuse in young adulthood. These facts make it clear that preventing bullying is important also for the sake of students who bully others.

And bystanders who witness bullying are affected as well. They often feel afraid at school, powerless to change the situation, and perhaps guilty for not taking action. Or they may be drawn into the bullying themselves and feel bad about it afterward. All of this may gradually change the group or classroom attitudes and norms in a harsher, less empathetic direction.

For a Healthy School Climate

When a school allows bullying to continue, the entire school climate is affected. The environment can become one of fear and disrespect, hampering the ability of students to learn. Students may feel insecure and tend not to like school very well. When students don't see the adults at school acting to prevent or intervene in bullying situations, they may feel that teachers and other school staff have little control over the students and don't care what happens to them.

For the Larger Community

The effects of bullying are so devastating and profound that over the last few years at least thirty (at the time of publication) state laws against bullying have been adopted. In addition to a general concern for student safety and well-being, some of the motivation for passing these laws includes the perception that a number of school shootings have been carried out by students who felt bullied, excluded, or threatened by their peers. The effects of these violent incidents on students, families, schools, and entire communities are felt long after the traumatic events occurred. The community as a whole benefits when students like school and have a variety of community settings where they feel they belong.

I really think our school's bullying prevention program has stopped the ugly bullying. I used to get glares from some kids and they wouldn't let me play with them. I'm glad that's changed!

— AN ELEMENTARY STUDENT

For the Purposes of Risk Management for Schools

There have also been civil suits brought against schools and school systems over bullying incidents, some with damages in the millions of dollars. It is important to realize that, like sexual harassment and racial discrimination, some forms of bullying are illegal actions and must be treated as such.

This Teacher Guide will give you the information you need to effectively implement the *Olweus Bullying Prevention Program.* Your efforts and the efforts of other staff in your school can have a profound impact on one of the most difficult issues students face today—bullying.

•　　•　　•

The biggest change with our students after going through the *Olweus Bullying Prevention Program* is they now know how to care for one another.

— AN ELEMENTARY SCHOOL COUNSELOR

You know, we kids can work on this, but it takes teachers that really care.

— AN ELEMENTARY STUDENT

Introducing the *Olweus Bullying Prevention Program*

WHAT YOU WILL LEARN IN CHAPTER 1	• the components of *OBPP* • the history and research behind the program • what resources are available to help you in its implementation

What Is the Olweus Bullying Prevention Program?

As stated earlier, the *Olweus Bullying Prevention Program (OBPP)* is the most researched and best-known bullying prevention program available today. With over thirty-five years of research and successful implementation all over the world, *OBPP* is a whole-school program that has been proven to prevent or reduce bullying throughout a school setting.

OBPP is used at the school, classroom, and individual levels and includes methods to reach out to parents and the community for involvement and support. School administrators, teachers, and other staff are primarily responsible for introducing and implementing the program. These efforts are designed to improve peer relations and make the school a safer and more positive place for students to learn and develop.

What Are the Goals of *OBPP?*

The goals of the program are

- to reduce existing bullying problems among students
- to prevent the development of new bullying problems
- to achieve better peer relations at school

For Whom Is *OBPP* Designed?

OBPP is designed for students in elementary, middle, and junior high schools (students age five to fifteen years old). All students participate in most aspects of the program, while students identified as bullying others, or as targets of bullying, receive additional individualized interventions.

With some adaptation, the program can also be used in high schools, although research has not measured the program's effectiveness beyond tenth grade.

What Are the *OBPP* Materials?

Teacher Guide

This Teacher Guide, with accompanying DVD and CD-ROM, serves as the primary program implementation tool for teachers and other classroom support staff. It highlights the important role you will play both in the classroom and in schoolwide efforts in preventing and addressing bullying. All the resources you need to implement the program, except for the Olweus Bullying Questionnaire, are provided in this guide or on the accompanying DVD and CD-ROM.

Ideally, every teacher should have a copy of this guide. If this is not possible, we recommend that each Teacher Guide be shared among no more than three teachers. (If at any time you need to reorder a Teacher Guide, contact Hazelden Publishing at 1-800-328-9000 or 1-651-213-4000.)

Schoolwide Guide

OBPP is used both in individual classrooms and throughout your school. It will be important that you participate at both levels. For the schoolwide effort, a Schoolwide Guide, with accompanying DVD and CD-ROM, is available to provide step-by-step instructions on how to implement the program in the entire school setting.

The power of the *Olweus Bullying Prevention Program* lies in staff and students using common language to address bullying situations. A message is carried out to students saying bullying will not be tolerated here.

— A JUNIOR HIGH SCHOOL COUNSELOR

The Schoolwide Guide is used mainly by your school's Bullying Prevention Coordinating Committee, the group that is established to guide schoolwide implementation. However, the Teacher Guide you are now reading does provide an overview of the schoolwide components in which you will participate.

Olweus Bullying Questionnaire

The Olweus Bullying Questionnaire is administered to all students in grades 3–12 before the program begins and at regular intervals (ideally each year) from then on. Your schoolwide program leaders coordinate the implementation of this questionnaire.

If you teach grades K–2, you will not administer the Olweus Bullying Questionnaire because the reading and conceptual levels are beyond that of most young students. However, if you would like to use the questionnaire with students in grades K–2, we recommend that your school's Bullying Prevention Coordinating Committee consult with your certified Olweus trainer about the best way to do this.

What Are the Components of the Program?

OBPP is not a classroom curriculum. It is a whole-school, systems-change program at four different levels. Here are the program components for each of these levels. Each component is discussed in more detail in later chapters.

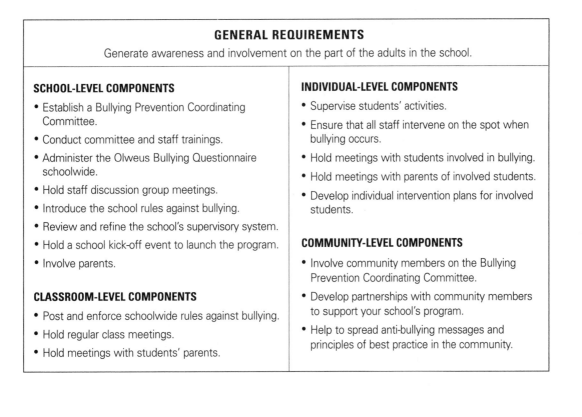

GENERAL REQUIREMENTS
Generate awareness and involvement on the part of the adults in the school.

SCHOOL-LEVEL COMPONENTS

- Establish a Bullying Prevention Coordinating Committee.
- Conduct committee and staff trainings.
- Administer the Olweus Bullying Questionnaire schoolwide.
- Hold staff discussion group meetings.
- Introduce the school rules against bullying.
- Review and refine the school's supervisory system.
- Hold a school kick-off event to launch the program.
- Involve parents.

CLASSROOM-LEVEL COMPONENTS

- Post and enforce schoolwide rules against bullying.
- Hold regular class meetings.
- Hold meetings with students' parents.

INDIVIDUAL-LEVEL COMPONENTS

- Supervise students' activities.
- Ensure that all staff intervene on the spot when bullying occurs.
- Hold meetings with students involved in bullying.
- Hold meetings with parents of involved students.
- Develop individual intervention plans for involved students.

COMMUNITY-LEVEL COMPONENTS

- Involve community members on the Bullying Prevention Coordinating Committee.
- Develop partnerships with community members to support your school's program.
- Help to spread anti-bullying messages and principles of best practice in the community.

I think schools really find *OBPP* attractive because it's schoolwide. It involves all school staff, students, and even parents in bullying prevention.

— PREVENTION SPECIALIST

What Are the Effects of the *Olweus Bullying Prevention Program?*

OBPP has been more thoroughly evaluated than any other bullying prevention/reduction program so far. Six large-scale evaluations, involving more than 40,000 students, have documented results such as the following:[1]

- Average reductions by 20 to 70 percent in student reports of being bullied and bullying others. Peer and teacher ratings of bullying problems have yielded roughly similar results.
- Marked reductions in student reports of general antisocial behavior, such as vandalism, fighting, theft, and truancy.
- Clear improvements in classroom social climate, as reflected in students' reports of improved order and discipline, more positive social relationships, and more positive attitudes toward schoolwork and school.

For students in grades 4–7, most of the positive results can be seen after only eight months of intervention work, given reasonably good implementation of the program. For students in grades 8–10, it may take somewhat more time, maybe two years, to achieve equally good results.

The program design has also been influenced by detailed *OBPP* research on how teacher and school factors affect implementation of the program. Interested readers are referred to the article "Predicting Teachers' and Schools' Implementation of the Olweus Bullying Prevention Program: A Multilevel Study" by Jan Helge Kallestad and Dan Olweus.[2]

What Is the History behind the *Olweus Bullying Prevention Program?*

Although bullying problems among students have been around for centuries, it wasn't until the early 1970s that Dr. Dan Olweus initiated the first systematic research study in the world on these problems. The results were published in a Swedish book in 1973 and in the United States in 1978 under the title *Aggression in the Schools: Bullies and Whipping Boys.* For a considerable period of time, up to the early 1990s, there was very little attention to and research on the topic of bullying outside of Scandinavia.

In 1983, after three adolescent boys in northern Norway committed suicide, most likely as a consequence of severe bullying by peers, the country's Ministry of Education initiated a national campaign against bullying in schools. In that context, the first version of what has later become known as the *Olweus Bullying Prevention Program* was developed.

The program was carefully evaluated in a large-scale project involving 40,000 students from forty-two schools followed over a period of two and a half years.[3] The program has since been refined, expanded, and further evaluated with successful results in five additional large-scale projects in Norway. Since 2001, as part of the Norwegian government's plans for the prevention and reduction of delinquency and violence among children and youth, *OBPP* has been implemented on a large-scale basis in elementary and lower secondary schools throughout Norway.

Dr. Olweus has for a long time seen the phenomenon of bullying in the context of human rights.[4] As early as 1981, he proposed enacting a law against bullying in schools. He argued that it is a fundamental human right for a student to feel safe in school and to be spared the repeated humiliation implied in bullying. In the mid-1990s, these arguments led to legislation against bullying by the Swedish and Norwegian parliaments. Similar legislation has been adopted in more than thirty states (at the date of publication) in the United States and in several other countries.

During the 1990s, Dr. Olweus worked closely with American colleagues, notably Dr. Susan P. Limber, now at Clemson University in South Carolina, to implement and evaluate the program in the United States, also resulting in positive though somewhat weaker outcomes. Since then, hundreds of schools in most every state in the United States have used the program, and the number is growing. Additional studies of these efforts are being conducted by the authors of this guide and other researchers. For summaries and citations of this research, visit www.clemson.edu/olweus.

At our school, we have seen amazing results after the first year—
increased attendance, increased student achievement,
and decreased incidents that lead to suspensions.

— ELEMENTARY MATH AND SCIENCE COORDINATOR

Is the *Olweus Bullying Prevention Program* a Nationally Recognized Program?

The *Olweus Bullying Prevention Program* has received recognition from a number of organizations including the following:

- Blueprints Model Program, Center for the Study and Prevention of Violence, University of Colorado at Boulder
  www.colorado.edu/cspv/blueprints/model/programs/BPP.html

- Model Program, Substance Abuse and Mental Health Services Administration, U.S. Department of Health and Human Services
  www.modelprograms.samhsa.gov

- Effective Program, Office of Juvenile Justice and Delinquency Prevention, U.S. Department of Justice
  www.ojjdp.ncjrs.org

- Level 2 Program, U.S. Department of Education
  www.helpingamericasyouth.gov

  Note: "Level 2" programs have been scientifically demonstrated to prevent delinquency or reduce risk and enhance protection for delinquency and other child and youth problems using either an experimental or quasi-experimental research design, with a comparison group.

For more information about the authors and other awards received for their work, see About the Authors on pages 127–129. For more information on the research behind the program, see the list of research articles provided on the Teacher Guide CD-ROM.

What Type of Support Is Available as You Implement the Program in Your Classroom?

OBPP is a program that is implemented throughout the entire school setting. As a classroom teacher, you will have a variety of responsibilities for this implementation, including supervising students in and outside of the classroom, teaching and talking with students about bullying, and intervening in bullying

The *Olweus Bullying Prevention Program* is one of the few programs
that seems to energize staff as opposed to making it feel like it is
"one more expectation or one more burden."

— SCHOOL PRINCIPAL

situations in your classroom and elsewhere in the school. Because these tasks are crucial to the success of *OBPP* in your school, it is important that you feel supported in your efforts. If you have any questions or concerns, take advantage of the following resources:

- **Your School's Bullying Prevention Coordinating Committee**

  A committee made up of school staff, administrators, teachers, and parents has most likely been established at your school to oversee the program. Committee members have been trained in the implementation of *OBPP* and can serve as a resource to you. Don't be afraid to ask questions or request that a committee member serve as a guide in your classroom as you get started.

- **Staff Discussion Groups**

  Your school will likely establish one or more staff discussion groups for classroom teachers and other staff. These groups meet with some regularity; there you can learn more about the program and its use at your school as well as discuss potential challenges to using *OBPP,* possible solutions, and other related topics in a safe context. Take advantage of this opportunity by participating regularly.

- **Your Certified Olweus Trainer**

  Most likely your school has contracted with an outside certified Olweus trainer or has had a staff member certified as an Olweus trainer. This person will have a wealth of knowledge about the program and is available for ongoing consultation via telephone and/or Internet contact (or in person, whenever possible) with your school administrator, your school's OBPP coordinator, and members of your Bullying Prevention Coordinating Committee. Check with a committee member about how to raise questions and concerns with this trainer.

- ***Olweus Bullying Prevention Program* Web Site**

  www.clemson.edu/olweus

  This Web site provides background information about the program, implementation strategies, training information, current evaluation research, and other related resources.

- **Hazelden Publishing Web Site**

  www.hazelden.org/olweus

  This Web site provides background information about the program and specific information about purchasing program materials.

* * *

2

Recognizing the
Many Faces of Bullying

WHAT YOU WILL LEARN IN CHAPTER 2	<ul><li>the definition of bullying</li><li>the different forms and possible types of bullying</li><li>the prevalence of bullying problems in general</li><li>the characteristics of students who are bullied and students who bully others</li><li>the roles students may take in a bullying situation</li></ul>

Although you are not expected to be an "expert" on the subject of bullying, it is very important that you, as a classroom teacher, have a basic understanding of what bullying is and how it affects students. This will help you more effectively implement the *Olweus Bullying Prevention Program* in your classroom. This chapter provides this basic information.

You can share much of this information with students during your class meetings, as described in chapter 6. For younger students, you will want to share only the information that seems age appropriate and relevant to their experiences.

Note: Throughout this guide we have been careful to avoid using the terms "bully" and "victim" as much as possible when describing students who bully others or who are bullied by others. This is intentional, and we encourage you to avoid these labels as well, when talking with your students. However, you may notice that such terms are often used in research literature as a convenient way to describe bullying situations. In this chapter (which shares current research on bullying) and a few other places, we will occasionally use these terms to facilitate the reading of the text.

Why Should You Address Bullying in Your Classroom?

Some more stories about bullying . . .

KELLY'S STORY

Kelly, age fourteen, was a new student at a middle school. Although she'd had quite a few good friends at her old school, she felt isolated and lonely among her new classmates. For reasons she didn't understand, she was on the "outs" with several popular girls and boys in her classes. At school, they rolled their eyes and snickered whenever she tried to speak up in class, barred her from their lunch table, and taped lewd notes and drawings of her on her locker. For Kelly, the final straw came when a classmate took an unflattering picture of her on his cell phone and forwarded it to most of the students in their class with the subject heading "Ugliest girl in school!"

JOHN'S STORY

John was bullied by some of his peers over the course of six years beginning in the first grade. Classmates called him "queer" and "sissy," threw paper at him, broke his pencils, ripped his school papers, knocked him down, and even punched him in the head in the presence of a teacher. John became so afraid that he refused to use the school bathroom. Teachers took little action against the students who bullied, and the principal suggested that John discourage the perpetrators by getting involved in sports. School officials monitored John for two weeks, but the behavior continued until his parents enrolled John in a private school.

A LETTER FROM A MOTHER OF A STUDENT WHO WAS BULLIED

It is agonizing to see your own child being bullied in school. My daughter, who is only nine years old, has already suffered terribly from bullying. Time after time, my daughter has come home from school feeling like an outcast. She says, "I hate school," and begs me not to make her go back.

Just during the last year, she has reported that many of the girls in her class sneer at her, or worse, completely ignore her. Someone wrote nasty messages about her in the girl's bathroom. And almost every other day someone puts taunting notes in her backpack that include calling her names like "stupid" or "ugly."

When girls are bullied by other girls, it often isn't easily visible from the outside, and it can be harder to recognize than physical bullying. While physical bullying can leave telltale signs like ripped clothing or bruises, relational or emotional bullying may leave no tangible signs. Bullying among girls often bypasses physical pain and goes directly to the soul. My daughter started school as a beautiful, happy, healthy girl who was eager to learn. These days she comes home from school feeling scared, insecure, and angry.

In desperation, I have talked to school staff and even parents of the students responsible for the bullying, but the bullying never stops. I feel powerless to help my daughter. If other parents and teachers would put themselves in my shoes and feel how serious bullying is when it's *their* child, then maybe we could work together to make our school a safer place for all children.

— A DESPAIRING MOTHER

Behind every story about bullying there is a story of pain and fear. Bullying takes a tremendous toll on students who are bullied, emotionally and often also physically. The above stories show how merciless and cruel students can be.

As we define bullying and explore statistics on its nature and prevalence, it is very important to keep in mind that behind every fact there is a hurting student who may be impacted for life by the bullying. In addition, there are bystanders or witnesses to the bullying who may be negatively affected by what they see.

It is also important to realize that for every case of bullying reported to school officials, there are many more cases that are never reported. Many bullied students suffer in silence.

To gain a clear sense of the emotional toll of bullying, we encourage you to watch the bullying scenarios on the Teacher Guide DVD. Also read and reflect on Maria's Story, found on the Teacher Guide CD-ROM. This story is based on an actual newspaper report that gives more detailed information on the nature and development of a bullying problem.

What Is the Definition of Bullying?

In order to address the issue of bullying, it is important to understand what bullying is. Here is a commonly used definition:

> A person is bullied when he or she is exposed, repeatedly and over time,
> to negative actions on the part of one or more other persons, and
> he or she has difficulty defending himself or herself.[1]

Expressed in more everyday language, one might say: Bullying is when someone repeatedly and on purpose says or does mean or hurtful things to another person who has a hard time defending himself or herself.

Duplicating this page is illegal. Do not duplicate without publisher's written permission.

11

The definition of bullying has three major components: First, it is aggressive behavior that involves unwanted, negative actions. Second, bullying typically involves a pattern of behavior repeated over time. Finally, it involves an imbalance of power or strength. We will examine each of these components in more detail below.

Bullying Is an Intentional, Negative Act

It is a negative act when someone intentionally inflicts injury or discomfort upon another person. The student or students who bully mean to harm another student in some way. This could be through physical actions, through words, or indirectly, for example, by intentionally excluding the student from a group or activity.

It is important to realize that a lot of bullying occurs without any apparent provocation on the part of the bullied student. Rather, students who bully usually take the initiative (use proactive aggression) and seek out students they perceive as weaker. A possible exception may be situations involving a "provocative victim" (discussed later in this chapter) where the students who are bullying may be reacting to disruptive behavior on the part of the targeted student.

Although students who bully others may vary in their awareness of how the targeted student perceives their actions, most or all of them likely realize that their behavior is at least somewhat painful or unpleasant.

Bullying Is Usually Repeated Behavior

Although bullying is defined as usually being carried out "repeatedly and over time," it would be wrong to exclude from the definition serious hurtful behavior that happens only once. The intent in focusing on repeated acts is to exclude nonserious actions that are directed at a student one time.

However, while bullying typically is repeated behavior, it may be difficult for adults to recognize that a "one-time" incident is part of a pattern of repeated behavior. This may be due to a number of reasons, including the fact that students who bully tend to be good at concealing or covering their behavior. Students who are bullied may also be embarrassed to tell an adult, or they may feel they won't get the help they need if they do report the bullying.

Bullying is when someone says or does mean things to another person.

— KINDERGARTEN STUDENT

While it is essential to understand that bullying happens repeatedly over time, it is not wise (and may even be dangerous) to wait for a pattern to clearly emerge before intervening. You need to respond anytime you observe or become aware of bullying or other related negative behaviors.

Bullying Involves a Power Imbalance

In a bullying situation or relationship, the student who is exposed to the negative actions has difficulty defending himself or herself and is somewhat helpless against the student or students who are doing the bullying.

The actual or perceived imbalance in power or strength may come about in several different ways. The student who is being bullied may actually be physically weaker or may simply perceive himself or herself as physically or emotionally weaker than the students who are bullying. Or there may be a difference in numbers, with several students ganging up on a single student.

A somewhat different kind of imbalance may happen when the "source" of the negative actions is difficult to identify or confront, as in social exclusion from the group, hurtful gossip that happens behind the student's back, or when a student is being sent anonymous mean notes.

> It is not bullying if there is conflict or aggression between students who are of equal power, whether that be the same physical or mental strength, or social status.

There is also a difference between bullying and teasing. In the everyday social interactions among peers in school, there occurs a good deal of (often repeated) teasing of a playful and relatively friendly nature; in most cases this cannot be considered bullying.

On the other hand, when repeated teasing is degrading and offensive and continues in spite of clear signs from the targeted student that he or she would like it to stop, this certainly qualifies as bullying. It is helpful to keep in mind this difference between friendly, playful teasing and bullying, although the line between them may sometimes appear somewhat blurred. (We will discuss the distinction between bullying, rough-and-tumble play, and real fighting later in this chapter.)

What Are the Different Forms or Kinds of Bullying?

There are several different forms of bullying. In the Olweus Bullying Questionnaire that you will administer to your students, there are two general or global questions about being bullied and bullying others, and questions about the following nine specific forms of bullying:

- being verbally bullied

- being socially excluded or isolated

- being physically bullied

- being bullied through lies and false rumors

- having money or other things taken or damaged

- being threatened or forced to do things

- racial bullying

- sexual bullying

- cyber-bullying (via cell phone or the Internet)

The Olweus Bullying Questionnaire asks students whether they have been bullied in these nine ways and whether they have bullied other students in these ways.

Direct and Indirect Forms of Bullying

It is possible to divide the different types of bullying into direct and indirect forms. In direct forms, bullying involves relatively open attacks, usually in a face-to-face confrontation. Typical examples of direct bullying include verbal bullying with derogatory comments and nasty names, and physical bullying with hitting, kicking, shoving, and spitting.

In indirect bullying, the aggressive acts are more concealed and subtle, and it may be more difficult for the bullied student to know who is responsible for the bullying. Typical examples include social isolation—that is, intentionally excluding someone from a group or activity—and spreading lies and nasty rumors.

Several forms of cyber-bullying may also be considered indirect in the sense that nasty messages are delivered from a distance and not in a face-to-face way. And in some cases, it may be difficult or almost impossible to find out who originally sent the message.

Relational or Social Bullying

Other terms that have been used to describe bullying are the somewhat overlapping concepts of relational bullying and social bullying. These are behaviors that are intended to damage a student's reputation or social standing with peers, and/or use the threat of loss of the relationship to manipulate others. Included in these categories are usually aggressive behaviors that involve social exclusion or isolation, spreading of rumors, and manipulation of friendships.

To get a sense of the level of relational or social bullying in your school, combine the results of the questions on social isolation and spreading of rumors on the Olweus Bullying Questionnaire.

Bullying, Rough-and-Tumble Play, or Real Fighting—What Is the Difference?

Our discussion on the different forms of bullying and its definition would not be complete without briefly considering two other categories of behavior that are sometimes mistaken for bullying: rough-and-tumble play and real fighting.

The Teacher Guide CD-ROM includes a table outlining how these three behaviors differ or are similar in such characteristics as the relationship between the participants, the balance of power between them, and the intent of the action.

The term "rough-and-tumble play" is normally used when two or more students hit, push, threaten, chase, or try to wrestle with each other in a friendly, nonhostile, playful manner. Research has shown that, even at an early age (about five years), students usually can differentiate between rough-and-tumble play and real fighting.[2] Students may say, "It's fun," "I like it," "It makes me laugh," as the most common reasons for participating in rough-and-tumble play. It is relatively rare for rough-and-tumble play to develop into real fighting.

Rough-and-tumble play differs from bullying and fighting with regard to the "relationship between the parties" and the "expression and atmosphere." Those who participate in rough-and-tumble play are usually friends and like each other, and this is expressed in more positive attitudes, atmosphere, and the nature of the interaction.

The major difference between real fighting and bullying, which can also include a real, but usually uneven fight, concerns the repeated nature of the behavior and the balance of power. "Real" fighting is often a one-time event between two parties of reasonably equal strength or power.

It can be difficult to determine if a situation is rough-and-tumble play, real fighting, or bullying. For example, it is possible that a fight may actually be caused by bullying that has been going on for a long time, and the bullied student has suddenly struck back at his or her tormenters. Or, an episode that both parties claim is "fun" or "innocent play" may actually be bullying.

For these and other reasons, you may want to prohibit any of these behaviors in your classroom or on school grounds, whether they are actually rough-and-tumble play, fighting, or bullying. It is also very important that you and other staff intervene immediately to stop any inappropriate or suspicious behavior, even

Duplicating this page is illegal. Do not duplicate without publisher's written permission.

15

though it sometimes may not be aggressive in nature but rather a somewhat noisy but basically friendly interaction.

It is important to remember that, just like sexual, racial, or disability harassment, bullying that is not properly addressed can have legal implications. School districts and school personnel can be held legally liable for the consequences of bullying.

How Much Bullying Is There in Today's Schools?

The first data on the prevalence of bullying in schools was collected in Norway by Dr. Dan Olweus. This large-scale, nationally representative study of bullying was done in 1983 with more than 40,000 students age eight to sixteen. This study found that 15 percent of children and youth reported that they had been regularly involved in bullying problems.[3] This represents one out of every seven students. Nine percent had been bullied, 7 percent had bullied other students, and less than 1.5 percent had been both bullied and bullied others.

A later (2001) large-scale Norwegian survey of 11,000 students from fifty-four elementary and junior high schools gave much the same picture as before but with two disturbing trends: (1) The percentage of bullied students had increased by approximately 50 percent from 1983 to 2001; and, (2) the percentage of students who were involved in the most frequent (and serious) form of bullying had increased by 65 percent.[4]

OBPP researchers and others have also conducted studies to determine how prevalent bullying is in the United States. In a study of 6,500 students in grades 4–6 in rural South Carolina, *OBPP* researchers found that 23 percent had been bullied "several times" or more within a school term, and 20 percent had bullied others.[5]

In the first nationally representative U.S. study of bullying, comprising more than 15,000 students in grades 6–10, 17 percent of students reported having been bullied "sometimes" or more often during the school term, and 8 percent had been bullied at least once a week. Nineteen percent had bullied others "sometimes" or more often during the term, and 9 percent had bullied other students at least once a week.[6]

It should be emphasized that the data from these studies are average estimates that do not highlight the great variation between different schools. Within the same community/school district, one school may experience bullying problems at a level two or three times higher than that of another school.[7]

Although the levels of bullying problems are higher in the United States than in Norway, the general pattern is quite similar. And it should be emphasized that national differences in bullying levels must be interpreted cautiously, since students' responses may be affected by cultural differences in their familiarity with the concept of bullying, the degree of public attention surrounding bullying, and legislation.

A general conclusion from the above studies is that bullying is a significant problem in both countries (actually in most countries studied so far) and a problem that affects very large numbers of students.

Bullying Problems by Grade and Gender

Most studies in Norway and the United States have found that the percentage of students who reported being bullied decreased with age/grade (see figure 1). It is the younger and weaker students who are most often bullied. There is also a clear trend toward less use of physical forms of bullying in the higher grades. Although a majority of targeted students are bullied by students at the same grade level, a significant amount of bullying is carried out by older students. This was particularly true of students who are bullied in the lower grades.[8]

Figure 1

Percentage of Students Who Reported Being Bullied at Least 2 or 3 Times a Month

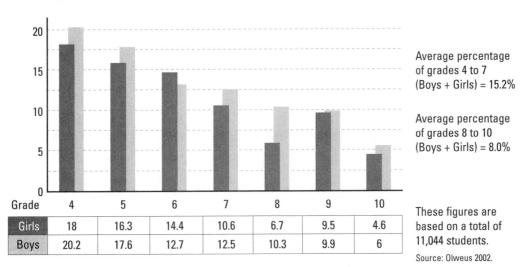

Average percentage of grades 4 to 7 (Boys + Girls) = 15.2%

Average percentage of grades 8 to 10 (Boys + Girls) = 8.0%

Grade	4	5	6	7	8	9	10
Girls	18	16.3	14.4	10.6	6.7	9.5	4.6
Boys	20.2	17.6	12.7	12.5	10.3	9.9	6

These figures are based on a total of 11,044 students.
Source: Olweus 2002.

Although not all studies have shown the same trend, generally there is an increase in the number of students who bully others at higher grades, in particular for boys, as shown in figure 2 on the next page.

As evident from figure 1, studies have also shown a tendency for boys to be somewhat more likely to be bullied than girls. This tendency is particularly true in the higher grades.

Figure 2

Percentage of Students Who Reported Bullying Others at Least 2 or 3 Times a Month

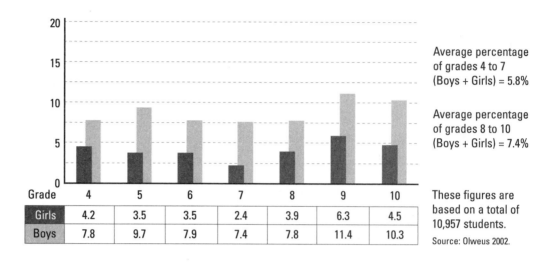

Average percentage of grades 4 to 7 (Boys + Girls) = 5.8%

Average percentage of grades 8 to 10 (Boys + Girls) = 7.4%

These figures are based on a total of 10,957 students.

Source: Olweus 2002.

Grade	4	5	6	7	8	9	10
Girls	4.2	3.5	3.5	2.4	3.9	6.3	4.5
Boys	7.8	9.7	7.9	7.4	7.8	11.4	10.3

Figure 2 shows the percentage of students who had regularly taken part in bullying other students. It is evident that a larger percentage of boys had participated in bullying other students. For the higher grades, it is a common result that two to four times as many boys as girls report having bullied other students.

Bullying by physical means is more common among boys. In contrast, girls often use more subtle and indirect forms of bullying, such as social exclusion, spreading rumors, and manipulation of friendships. Nonetheless, bullying with nonphysical means—by words, in particular—is usually the most common form of bullying among both boys and girls.

An additional finding is that boys carry out a large part of the bullying to which girls are subjected. In the Norwegian studies, more than 50 percent of bullied girls reported being bullied mainly by boys. Only 25 percent of the bullied girls were bullied by other girls. An additional 25 percent reported that they were bullied by both boys and girls. The great majority of boys, on the other hand—more than 80 percent—were bullied primarily by boys.

Another consistent and important finding has been that most of the bullying in school is carried out by a small group of two or three students, often with a negative leader. However, 25 to 35 percent of bullied students report that they are mainly bullied by a single student.

In summary, boys are somewhat more often targets and in particular perpetrators of bullying. This conclusion is consistent with research on gender differences in aggressive behavior. It is well documented that relations among boys are by and large harder, tougher, and more aggressive than among girls.[9]

The results presented here should by no means imply that we do not need to pay attention to bullying problems among girls. Bullying problems among girls must be acknowledged and counteracted, whether girls are the targets of bullying or they are bullying others. No doubt, being bullied in indirect and subtle ways (the more common types of bullying done by girls) can be equally hurtful and damaging as being bullied in more open and direct ways.

An Overview of the Causes of Bullying Problems

The extensive research evidence collected so far clearly suggests that personality characteristics or typical reaction patterns, in combination with physical strength or weakness in the case of boys, are important factors for the development of bullying problems in individual students. At the same time, environmental factors such as the attitudes, routines, and behavior of relevant adults—in particular teachers and principals—play a major role in determining the extent to which the problems will manifest themselves in a larger unit such as a classroom or a school. The attitudes and behavior of relevant peers as revealed in group processes and mechanisms are certainly also important. As a result, analyses of the causes of bullying problems must be pursued on several different levels.

What Are the Characteristics of Students Who Are Bullied?

When we talk about the characteristics of students who are involved in bullying problems, it is important to realize that we are focusing on main tendencies. Individual students may vary a lot. With regard to being bullied, almost any student can become a target under certain circumstances. An important general factor is, of course, whether there are aggressive peers in the classroom or group the student belongs to.[10]

There are two main types of bullied students. In the research literature they have been called "submissive victims" or "passive victims" (victims only) and "provocative victims" or "bully-victims" (those who both are bullied and bully others).

Note: Although the research literature describes these students as "submissive," "passive," or "provocative," these labels are not meant to be pejorative or in any way blame these students for the bullying they experience.

Submissive Victims

Submissive victims are students who are bullied, but do not bully others in return or do not provoke the bullying. However, using the term "submissive" or "passive" does not mean the student willingly accepts the bullying. Submissive victims are much more common than provocative victims who both bully others and are bullied.[11]

Students in the submissive category usually have one or more of the following characteristics. They

- are cautious, sensitive, quiet, withdrawn, and shy
- are anxious, insecure, unhappy, and have low self-esteem
- are depressed and engage in suicidal ideation much more often than their peers
- often do not have a single good friend and relate better to adults than to peers
- are often physically weaker than their peers (if they are boys) and in particular, weaker than those who bully

It should be noted that such characteristics have been identified in research on children and youth who already have been bullied for some time. This means that the picture one gets of them is likely to be, at least in part, a result of the negative treatment to which they have been exposed. All things considered, it is reasonable to assume that some characteristics, such as cautiousness and sensitivity, may have contributed to their becoming targets of bullying. At the same time, it is obvious that the repeated harassment by peers must have considerably increased their anxiety, depression, insecurity, and generally negative evaluation of themselves. Some of the listed characteristics are thus likely to be both causes and consequences of bullying.[12]

Students who are bullied may develop physical symptoms such as headaches, stomach pains, or sleeping problems. They may be afraid to go to school, go to the bathroom, or ride the school bus. They may also lose interest in school, have trouble concentrating, and do poorly academically.

Bullied students typically lose confidence in themselves and start to think of themselves as stupid, a failure, or unattractive. They may even develop feelings of guilt for being bullied ("there must be something wrong with me since I am the one being bullied"). Although relatively rare, some students who have been bullied repeatedly attempt and actually commit suicide.[13]

The effects of being bullied typically do not end in childhood. *OBPP* research has shown that boys who were bullied during the junior high school years were likely to suffer from depression and low self-esteem seven to ten years after most of the bullying stopped. The results suggest that their problems in young adulthood were largely a consequence of the bullying they had experienced many years before.[14]

Provocative Victims or Bully-Victims

The other, smaller group, comprising only 10 to 20 percent of bullied students, is the "provocative victims," also called "bully-victims." These students both are bullied and bully others.

As with bullied students in the submissive victim category, these students may be depressed, socially anxious, lack positive self-esteem, and be socially isolated and feel disliked by peers. Also, as with submissive victims, the number of provocative victims decreases as students get older.

However, provocative victims also show similarities with students who bully others by displaying more dominant, aggressive, and antisocial behavior and having more problems with concentration, hyperactivity, and impulsivity (ADHD). They try to bully weaker students, although they may be less effective than "pure" bullies (who are not themselves bullied). There are more boys (in a ratio of two or three to one) in this category than girls, which is also true for students who bully others. In addition, these students may have reading and writing problems.[15]

Although these students are called provocative victims, there is nothing to indicate that they want to actively provoke others or to be bullied. Rather, they behave in ways that may cause tension, irritation, and negative reactions from their classmates and often also from their teacher.

How you deal with a problem involving a provocative victim in the classroom is likely different from how you handle a problem involving a submissive victim. For example, you may need to help a provocative victim learn better ways to interact with his or her peers, without implying that the bullying is his or her fault. No matter how students behave, other students should not feel justified in responding with bullying.

Remember that provocative victims represent a small percentage of students who are bullied, although they attract a good deal of negative attention through their behavior.

What Are the Characteristics of Students Who Bully Others?

Students who bully other students (pure bullies) are likely to have several of the following characteristics:[16]

- have a positive attitude toward violence and the use of violent means
- have strong needs to dominate and subdue other students and to get their own way
- are impulsive and easily angered

- show little empathy toward students who are bullied
- are defiant and aggressive toward adults, including teachers and parents
- are involved in other antisocial or rule-breaking activities such as vandalism, delinquency, and substance abuse
- if they are boys, they tend to be physically stronger than boys in general and particularly the students they bully
- are more likely to report owning a gun for risky reasons, such as to gain respect or to frighten others[17]

It is a common belief that students who bully others are tough on the outside and insecure and anxious on the inside. It is also believed that they have poor self-esteem and that this is the driving force behind their bullying. In line with this reasoning, if one only increases their self-esteem, they have no need to bully others and will stop such behavior.

However, these assumptions are not supported by evidence. *OBPP* research and other studies indicate that students who bully others tend to have little anxiety and uncertainty or are average in this respect. Their self-esteem is also about average or relatively positive.[18]

There is a wide range in the popularity of students who bully. Some are popular, others are not, and some are moderately popular. A student who takes the lead in bullying often has a group of two or three friends who support him or her and join in the bullying.

Bullying can also be viewed as part of an antisocial and rule-breaking behavior pattern. Students who bully others at school are more likely than other students to become involved in other problem behaviors such as criminality and substance abuse. One *OBPP* study found that by the age of twenty-four, boys who were identified as bullies in junior high school were four times more likely to have been convicted of three or more criminal acts than boys who did not bully others.[19]

Not all students who bully others have obvious behavior problems or are engaged in rule-breaking activities, however. Some of them are highly skilled socially and good at ingratiating themselves with their teacher and other adults. This is true of some boys who bully but is perhaps even more common among bullying girls. For this reason it is often difficult for adults to discover or even imagine that these students engage in bullying behavior.

Why Do Some Students Bully?

Research suggests at least three partly interrelated motives for bullying:

- Students who bully have strong needs for power and (negative) dominance; they seem to enjoy being "in control" and subduing others.

- Students who bully find satisfaction in causing injury and suffering to other students. This is at least partly due to the environment at home, which may have caused hostility within the student.

- Students who bully are often rewarded in some way for their behavior. This could be material or psychological rewards, such as forcing the student who is bullied to give them money or steal for them, or enjoying the attention, status, and prestige they are granted from other students because of their behavior.

As suggested above, students who bully others may have some common family characteristics, such as parents who are not very involved in their children's lives, who lack warmth and positive involvement. In addition, these parents may not have set clear limits on their children's aggressive behavior and have allowed them to act out aggressively toward their siblings and other children.

Parents of children who bully are also more likely to use physical punishments and other "power-assertive" methods of child rearing. In summary, too little love and care and too much "freedom" in childhood are conditions that contribute to bullying behavior.[20]

In addition, children who bully others are more likely to have witnessed or been involved in domestic violence.[21] In all probability, they have also been exposed or exposed themselves to violence in the media and may have participated in "power sports" like boxing, kickboxing, and wrestling.[22]

It is important to emphasize once more that we are talking about main trends. Not all children who come from families with these characteristics will bully others, and not all children who bully come from these family environments.

The peer group may also play an important role in motivating and encouraging bullying behavior in certain students. Peer roles and group mechanisms in bullying will be discussed below.

What Roles Do Students Play in Bullying Situations?

A bullying situation is not something that affects only the student who is bullied or the students who are doing the bullying. Nearly every student who is involved

Duplicating this page is illegal. Do not duplicate without publisher's written permission.

23

in or witnesses a bullying situation is affected.[23] In *OBPP*, students are seen as occupying various roles or positions in a conceptual scheme called the Bullying Circle.[24]

Here is a description of each role in the Bullying Circle:

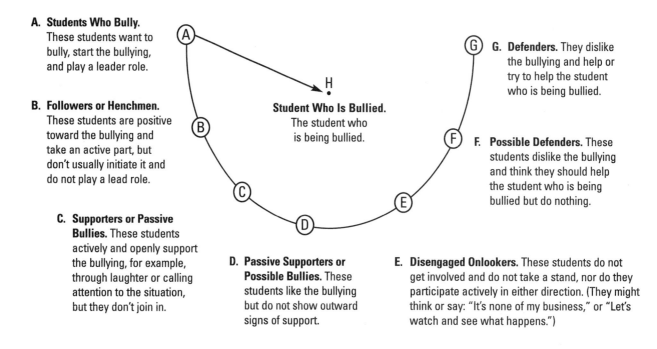

A. Students Who Bully. These students want to bully, start the bullying, and play a leader role.

B. Followers or Henchmen. These students are positive toward the bullying and take an active part, but don't usually initiate it and do not play a lead role.

C. Supporters or Passive Bullies. These students actively and openly support the bullying, for example, through laughter or calling attention to the situation, but they don't join in.

Student Who Is Bullied. The student who is being bullied.

D. Passive Supporters or Possible Bullies. These students like the bullying but do not show outward signs of support.

E. Disengaged Onlookers. These students do not get involved and do not take a stand, nor do they participate actively in either direction. (They might think or say: "It's none of my business," or "Let's watch and see what happens.")

F. Possible Defenders. These students dislike the bullying and think they should help the student who is being bullied but do nothing.

G. Defenders. They dislike the bullying and help or try to help the student who is being bullied.

The various roles in the Bullying Circle reflect two basic dimensions: the students' attitudes toward the bullying (positive, neutral, or negative) and their possible actions or behaviors (action or nonaction) toward the bullied students.

Students in roles from C (Supporters or Passive Bullies) to G (Defenders) may be considered bystanders. As evident from the description of these roles, a group of bystanders may represent very different attitudes and typical behaviors.

Research shows that the roles of Bullies, Followers or Henchmen, and Victims remain fairly stable over time (although Followers may sometimes lead the bullying), unless some type of intervention is done. The other roles are more flexible and may change depending on the situation.

An important goal of *OBPP* is to create anti-bullying norms in the peer group that will help to move students toward the right-hand side of the Bullying Circle, particularly into the role of a Defender of the bullied student.[25]

As a teacher, you can use the Bullying Circle to help students explore the various roles in a bullying situation, discuss motivations of the various actors, and look for possible solutions to each person's participation. You can do this, for example, through class meeting discussions or role-plays. More information on Bullying Circle activities for the classroom are discussed in chapter 6.

Group Mechanisms in Bullying

As indicated in the Bullying Circle, most students in a group are in some way affected by a bullying situation or problem. Sometimes almost all students in a class or group participate actively in the bullying of a particular student. This is most likely to occur when the targeted student is a provocative victim.

Bullying, therefore, is usually a group phenomenon even though some individuals play a much more active role than others. This explains why ordinarily positive/social and nonaggressive students now and then participate in bullying. Here are some of the group mechanisms at work.[26]

Social Contagion

Some students may be influenced to participate in the bullying if the student or students who take the lead are popular and perhaps admired. The bullying behavior may be "contagious" and spread particularly to students who are somewhat insecure and want to assert themselves in the group.

Weakening the Normal Inhibitions against Aggression

If the bullying is not stopped, students who bully others become the "winners" in these situations. Other students who would normally view bullying as wrong might join in, since they are not getting the message from adults and other students that this is, indeed, unacceptable behavior.

A Decreased Sense of Individual Responsibility

Students tend to feel less responsible or guilty if there are several students participating in a negative activity such as bullying. Students who would not usually be mean or bully others might join in bullying with a group and feel little responsibility for what happens. This mechanism is called "diffusion of responsibility" in social psychology.

Gradual Changes in the View of the Victim

Through repeated open attacks and derogatory comments, the bullied student is gradually almost "dehumanized" and viewed by other students as a worthless person who "asks to be bullied."

All of these group mechanisms work to reduce feelings of guilt and remorse in students who occasionally join in the bullying but who would otherwise not have taken an active part, as well as students who are more apt to be involved in bullying (roles A and B in the Bullying Circle).

It is an important goal of *OBPP* to counteract these group mechanisms and thereby increase all students' feelings of individual responsibility for what may happen in their peer group.

What Are Some Common Myths about Bullying?

There are some common views of bullying that are incorrect or only partly true. Research provides many facts about bullying that strongly contradict these myths. Take a look at the following statements and the research that addresses them:

Myth: Very Few Students Are Bullied.

As mentioned earlier in this chapter (page 16), a nationally representative U.S. study showed that 17 percent of all students reported having been bullied "sometimes" or more often within a school term. That is almost one in five students.[27]

Myth: Most Bullying Is Physical in Nature.

Physical bullying is relatively common among boys in lower grades; however, other forms of bullying, particularly verbal bullying, are more common among both boys and girls and across all grades.[28] See page 18 in this chapter.

Myth: Only Boys Bully.

Boys are more likely than girls to bully, but certainly this does not mean that girls don't bully or that their bullying can't be extremely harmful. Although boys bully both boys and girls, girls tend to bully other girls (unless they are in the company of boys, in which case they may sometimes also bully boys). Girls typically use more indirect forms of bullying, such as intentional exclusion from a group and spreading rumors and gossiping.[29]

Myth: Bullying Happens More Often Outside of School Than in School.

In a large-scale *OBPP* study in Norway and Sweden, almost twice as many students reported being bullied in school than on the way to and from school.[30] Similar results were obtained in U.S. studies.[31] Common locations for bullying at school include the playground and/or athletic fields (especially among elementary school children), the classroom, the lunchroom, hallways, and bathrooms.

Myth: Students Who Bully Others Are Anxious and Insecure and Have Low Self-Esteem.

OBPP research and other studies indicate that students who bully others typically have little anxiety and uncertainty (or at least are average in this respect). Their self-esteem is also about average or relatively positive.[32]

Myth: Bullying Is Mostly an Urban Problem.

Research with U.S. students has shown no marked differences in the levels of bullying problems in urban, suburban, town, and rural areas.[33] Similar results were obtained in the large-scale *OBPP* study with Norwegian students.[34]

Myth: Bullying Happens More Often in Large Schools and Large Classes.

Results from several studies have been inconclusive, typically reporting only weak or no relationships between the size of the school or the size of the class, on the one hand, and the levels of bullying problems on the other. In addition, it must be pointed out that even if a clear positive or negative relationship were consistently found, this would not prove that the heightened or reduced levels of problems were an effect of the size of the school or the class. It could, for example, be a reflection of factors related to the recruitment area of the school: Large schools may be particularly common in residential areas with many social problems including bullying.[35]

What Are Some Special Bullying Issues That You Should Be Aware Of?

Children with Behavior or Conduct Problems

A sizable number of students, and boys in particular, who frequently bully also have behavioral or conduct difficulties. However, it is important to note that students with behavior problems are not the only ones who bully.

Teachers have been surprised to find that students who are successful at school, who come from homes with no apparent problems, and who have no obvious conduct problems may bully others and be negative leaders of gullible friends.

Children with Disabilities, Special Needs, and Health Problems

Children with disabilities, special needs, or health problems are at increased risk of being bullied by other students. This includes students with cognitive and learning/behavioral disabilities, attention-deficit/hyperactivity disorder (ADHD) and Asperger's syndrome, medical conditions that affect their appearance, and other medical conditions such as diabetes, obesity, and stuttering. Some students with attention and hyperactivity problems (ADHD) are likely to be regarded as provocative victims. However, it must also be recognized that a sizable proportion of these students actually fall in the category of students who bully others.[36]

Bullying of students with disabilities and similar problems may be a civil-rights issue, and schools can be held legally responsible. For more information on federal disability harassment policies, visit www.ed.gov/about/offices/list/ocr/docs/disabharassltr.html.

Cyber-Bullying

Methods of bullying have evolved with technology. A wide variety of cyber technologies have provided children and youth new venues for bullying each other. In the United States, the most common type of cyber-bullying seems to be through instant messaging, where students send email or text messages with only a screen name for identification. As students have more access to cell phones, text messaging and cameras on cell phones are also being used to bully other students. Inappropriate information about students is also being posted on Web pages (for example, in blogs), chat rooms, and social networking sites (such as Myspace or Facebook).

One study found that 18 percent of middle school students had been cyber-bullied at least once in the previous two months, and 6 percent of them had been cyber-bullied two to three times a month or more often. Girls were twice as likely to cyber-bully than boys. Often the identity of the perpetrator was unknown or hidden.[37]

Since the phenomenon of cyber-bullying is quite new, it is difficult to know at this point to what extent research results on student behavior are dependent on relative access to and popularity of various technologies and on the cultural context. To illustrate this point, several (as yet unpublished) studies from England and Norway indicate that bullying via cell phones and over the Internet (in ways other than instant messaging) is much more common in these countries than bullying through instant messaging. In these studies, there were also no marked gender differences.

It is important for schools to be aware of and monitor closely the development of cyber-bullying in their schools. They should also include it in their anti-bullying efforts. For more information on cyber-bullying, see the fact sheet on the Teacher Guide CD-ROM.

Bullying Based on Sexual Orientation

GLBTQ (gay, lesbian, bisexual, transgender, or questioning) young people are often targets of bullying. A recent National Mental Health Association study found that 78 percent of gay (or believed to be gay) teens had been harassed in their school communities.[38] In a nationally representative sample of nearly 3,500 students in the United States ages thirteen through eighteen, one-third of the teens reported that students in their school were frequently harassed because of their perceived or actual sexual orientation.[39]

For more information on bullying issues related to sexual orientation, see the fact sheet on the Teacher Guide CD-ROM.

Teachers Who Bully

Although *OBPP* is focused on peer bullying with students as perpetrators and targets, it is important to realize that adults bully too. In a study by Dr. Dan Olweus of 2,400 Norwegian students in grades 7–10, it was found that about forty students, or somewhat less than 2 percent, could be identified as having been regularly bullied by one or (in a minority of cases) several teachers in the reference period of five months. This study, which is considered to be the first of its kind in the world, was based on student reports. To reduce the influence of nonserious or erratic responses from the students, the study used rather strict criteria for identification of a bullying teacher—a teacher who repeatedly behaved in arrogant, derogatory, and humiliating ways toward particular students. Although the percentage of students being bullied by teachers may be considered relatively low in comparison with the prevalence figures for students being bullied by peers, it was clearly higher than expected.[40]

In an anonymous survey of 116 elementary school teachers from seven schools in the United States, researchers found that one-third knew of one or more teachers who had bullied students in the past school year; 16 percent knew of two or more teachers who had done so. When asked if they could think of any times when they had themselves bullied a student, 40 percent indicated yes.[41]

These results show that the problem of teacher bullying of students deserves more attention. *OBPP* provides a common language about bullying that may help focus on possible problems with teachers bullying students and on bullying among adults in general. When it comes to identifying teacher bullying of students, you may find it useful to ask yourself if you have ever

- picked on or embarrassed a particular student in front of other students
- used humor or sarcastic comments to ridicule or make fun of a student
- played favorites with some students while treating others more harshly
- inappropriately used your power as a disciplinarian with students

Now that you have some background on the problem of bullying, you can move forward to the next chapter to see how you and your students can become part of the solution.

·   ·   ·

3

Supporting Schoolwide Implementation of the Program

WHAT YOU WILL LEARN IN CHAPTER 3	• the core principles of *OBPP* • what role classroom teachers play in the schoolwide implementation of the program • more about the schoolwide components of the program

Implementing the *Olweus Bullying Prevention Program* requires collaboration and communication among all members of a school staff. Although your main responsibility will be to implement the classroom components of *OBPP*, it is important to realize that the program is a schoolwide effort and you are a key player in integrating the program into all areas of your school, not just the classroom.

> You have an important role to play in implementing *OBPP* in all areas of your school, not just the classroom.

What Are the Core Principles behind the *Olweus Bullying Prevention Program?*

OBPP is based on a core set of guiding principles. These principles are derived chiefly from research on the development and modification of the problem behaviors implied in bullying, notably aggression or abuse toward peers. The overarching goal is to restructure the school environment in such a way as to markedly reduce both opportunities and rewards for bullying behavior.

It is important to develop a school environment characterized by the following core principles. Understanding and abiding by these core principles will help you implement *OBPP* with integrity and success. Here are the core principles:

- warmth, positive interest, and involvement by adults
- firm limits to unacceptable behavior

- consistent use of nonphysical, nonhostile negative consequences when rules are broken
- adults who function as authorities and positive role models

Let's look at each principle in more detail:

PRINCIPLE 1

Warmth, Positive Interest, and Involvement Are Needed on the Part of Adults in the School

Positive interest and involvement mean many things—taking time to know your students, making special efforts to help students with schoolwork, showing appropriate interest in students' personal lives, treating them with respect, and finding ways to praise them. The focus should be on developing a sense of community connection and caring, and praising the positive, supportive behavior of students, while addressing bullying situations in respectful ways.

With regard to praise, students are likely to repeat behaviors for which they have been praised. You can use many different forms of praise to let your students know you recognize their anti-bullying efforts and other positive behaviors, and that you care about them. Encouraging words, friendly smiles, pats on the shoulder—these are all ways to praise your students. More information about praise and the use of other positive consequences will be presented in chapter 5.

Being positive and respectful should not be limited to teacher-student interactions, either. Students need to see teachers and other adults in school treating each other this way as well. You are an important role model for students even when they aren't directly involved. Also, when teachers and other staff work cooperatively, it sets a tone of teamwork and unity in the building.

PRINCIPLE 2

Set Firm Limits to Unacceptable Behavior

Students need a clear understanding of what your school's anti-bullying rules are and the possible consequences for breaking them. Just presenting the rules isn't enough. They need to be clarified and thoroughly discussed. In addition, these rules need to be implemented with students at each grade level so that they understand in real-life terms what it means to follow the rules.

The *OBPP* rules will be introduced in chapter 5, and ideas about how to discuss the rules with students are outlined in chapter 6. Applying consequences is discussed in principle 3 on the next page and in chapter 5.

Also review the rules with students periodically to make sure students remember what they are and what they mean in concrete terms. Research suggests that students are less likely to follow rules if they are not able to summarize them in their own words. One possible positive reward in your classroom might be recognition for being able to explain the school's rules about bullying behavior.

PRINCIPLE 3

Consistently Use Nonphysical, Nonhostile Negative Consequences When Rules Are Broken

Students need to experience that the adults in your school will address bullying in roughly the same way, using the same rules and similar general guidelines for use of positive and negative consequences. This creates a schoolwide climate where bullying behaviors are unacceptable and assures students who are bullied that adults will take action to stop bullying.

Positive consequences alone will not usually get aggressive students to change their behavior. However, using physical or violent punishments has been shown to increase aggression in students. Several types of nonphysical negative consequences and how to use them are discussed in chapter 5.

PRINCIPLE 4

Adults in the School Should Function as Authorities and Positive Role Models

OBPP is based on an authoritative (not authoritarian) adult-student relationship model in which the adults are encouraged to be clear and visible authorities with responsibility for making sure a student's entire school experience is safe and positive. An authoritative leadership style implies a combination of positive interest and involvement on the one hand and clear expectations for appropriate behavior and firm limits to unacceptable behavior on the other.

Adults are important role models for students. As mentioned earlier in this chapter, the adults in the school need to model positive behavior toward each other and the students. When students see adults taking action against bullying behavior, it empowers them to do the same.

❖

A school environment that's safe helps kids come ready to learn, and maybe that's why our school [which uses *OBPP*] is one of the best ever.

— A MIDDLE SCHOOL STUDENT

Cooperation and teamwork between adults at school set up a model for students to follow and contribute to a positive, warm, and caring school environment. It is also important that the adults don't bully students by being sarcastic, derogatory, or disrespectful—abusing the power they have as teachers or other school staff.

What Are the Implications of These Principles?

Here are several important implications of these core principles:

1. **The main responsibility for bullying prevention and *OBPP* implementation rests with the adults in your school, not with students.**

   Adults should take primary responsibility for maintaining a safe learning environment. Students should not be expected to end or reduce bullying on their own; adults should take the lead in doing this. Appropriate action on the part of the adults reinforces your school's anti-bullying rules and sends a message that the adults at your school care about students and are in control.

2. **A clear, consistent message against bullying should be present throughout your school.**

   Adults in your school must be committed to the program's success. As a classroom teacher, you have a role in *OBPP* that extends beyond your classroom. It will be important for you and other staff to reinforce the anti-bullying message throughout your school.

3. **School staff must be focused on both short-term and long-term goals.**

   In the short term, teachers and other school staff can address bullying behavior as it occurs. But it is helpful to set long-term goals toward systemwide change. It is not uncommon for the number of reported bullying problems to increase in the short term when *OBPP* is first implemented. This is likely to be a positive sign, indicating that students are better able to recognize bullying and feel

The program also forces you to look at bullying in a different light, giving it a much more serious approach rather than something that kids just do. It really works to change attitudes toward bullying.

— A PREVENTION SPECIALIST

more comfortable reporting it. Many schools see positive results right away, but it may take a year to eighteen months after implementation for some schools to see a clear decline in bullying rates.

4. **Because *OBPP* is a research-based program, its procedures and guidelines should be followed as closely as possible.**

   In order to see the same significant results as were found in *OBPP* research studies, the program needs to be used with fidelity, meaning it needs to be implemented as closely as possible to the guidelines and concrete recommendations presented in this Teacher Guide and in the Schoolwide Guide.

5. ***OBPP* is designed to become part of the everyday life of a school.**

   Unlike a curriculum, *OBPP* is integrated into the daily procedures and processes of your school and classroom. In order to have its greatest impact, the program must become a natural part of everyday life in your school.

6. **Changing the school climate/school culture requires student involvement as well.**

   Although the primary responsibility for *OBPP* is in the hands of the adults, all students must become involved as well. Bullying is not just an issue for the students who bully and the students who are bullied. Bullying affects every student at school and all students have a role to play in changing the school climate.

   The Bullying Circle mentioned in chapter 2 describes the roles of bystanders in bullying. In order to change the school climate or school culture, bystanders—both students and adults—need to learn how they can affect a bullying situation. An important part of bullying prevention is helping students and adults realize that bullying is their business and that they need to help the student who is being bullied. Your students will learn about this message through class meetings and discussions.

   You will also want to reward students for their efforts in preventing or intervening in a bullying situation or for including students who are often excluded and might be likely targets of bullying. These positive steps help make your classroom and school a more pleasant place to be and a more positive place to learn.

7. Students need to be taught what bullying is and how to get help.

It cannot be assumed that your students fully understand what bullying is and how to get help when it happens. As the teacher, you need to teach them what bullying is, what the rules about bullying are, and what strategies they can use in seeking help for bullying problems.

As chapter 2 described, there are many different forms of bullying. Your students will need to understand that physical bullying is just one form and that other forms, such as verbal taunts, gossiping, name-calling, exclusion, and cyber-bullying, can be just as hurtful. Students need to understand that the rules apply to all forms of bullying behavior, even the more subtle and indirect kinds.

8. Bullying prevention and intervention are different from peer mediation or conflict resolution.

Because one of the main characteristics of bullying is an imbalance of power, it cannot be considered "normal" relational conflict between two students. Bullying is a form of peer abuse, and the student who is being bullied needs to be protected from such victimization. Because of the difference in power between the student or students who bully and the student who is being bullied, conflict resolution or peer mediation strategies should not be used to address bullying problems. Here are some more reasons why:

- Peer mediation/conflict resolution programs assume there is a bit of both right and wrong on both sides. Such programs may place some blame on the student who is being bullied and free the student or students who are bullying from some responsibility. These programs work toward a compromise that, in the case of bullying, could mean further victimization of the student who has been bullied.

- Another common assumption in such programs is that both parties have about the same negotiating power. This is usually not the case in bullying situations, where there is an imbalance in power in favor of the student or students who bully. Chances are the bullied student will be the loser in such negotiations.

- In peer mediation/conflict resolution programs, the mediator is told not to take a moral stand on the issue at hand. In the case of bullying, it is very important that the adults take a moral stand and clearly communicate that bullying is not acceptable.

• Peer mediation/conflict resolution programs leave most of the responsibility for solving bullying problems to the students. Such problems are often complex and difficult to handle, even for trained school staff. To defer these problems to the students is giving them too much responsibility. By using peer mediators, staff may also think that bullying is not their problem to solve.

9. *OBPP* **is not a classroom-management technique.**

Most aspects of good classroom management are certainly compatible with the principles of *OBPP*. Good classroom management helps set a positive tone in the classroom and school environment, and is likely to result in more efficient use of *OBPP* in the classroom. However, good classroom management will probably have rather limited effects on bullying problems, in and of itself.

One of the reasons for this is that many bullying problems occur outside of the classroom and your supervision. To effectively address bullying, you and your school must also use a number of measures specifically aimed at bullying problems, such as those in *OBPP*. By using *OBPP* in the classroom, you may see improvements in your classroom management.

What Are the Schoolwide Components of *OBPP*?

OBPP is composed of several schoolwide components in addition to classroom, individual, and community components. Together, these make up a comprehensive systemwide-change program that can reduce bullying in your school.

We briefly covered the program components in chapter 1. A more in-depth description follows. Again, you will want to be involved in these schoolwide efforts as much as possible, while being the primary implementer of the program in your classroom.

Here are the schoolwide components:

Bullying Prevention Coordinating Committee (BPCC)

This building-level committee is responsible for making sure all components of *OBPP* are implemented in your school. This includes coordinating the administration of the Olweus Bullying Questionnaire, providing training and program information to all teachers and other staff, coordinating *OBPP* with other programs and events in your school, obtaining feedback from staff about how the program is working, and representing the program to parents, the community, and the media.

The committee holds regular meetings, and one member of the committee usually acts as the coordinator of the program. Normally this committee is made up of the following individuals:

Committee Members	Role of This Member
A school administrator (principal or assistant principal)	Provides administrative leadership so the program is given priority in your school
A teacher at each grade level	Serves as a program liaison with other teachers in his or her grade, adapts the program to his or her grade level, and serves as a resource to other teachers
A school counselor and/or school-based mental health professional	Serves as a program liaison with other counselors and other school-based mental health professionals, sets up intervention processes, and provides referral information, if needed
A representative of the non-teaching staff (e.g., bus driver, cafeteria worker, custodian)	Serves as a program liaison to other members of his or her staff, reinforces *OBPP* rules and procedures, and applies the program in his or her area
One to two parents, depending on the size of the school	Promotes the program to parents, helps coordinate parent events, and gives a parent perspective to the committee
A representative from the community (if possible), such as after-school or youth program staff or representatives from the business or faith community who might have a stake in the results of the program	Promotes support of the program in the community, looks for ways to integrate the program into community efforts, and gives a community perspective
Other school personnel (e.g., nurse, school resource officer) who may bring particular expertise to the committee	Determine how to apply the program to their areas, provide unique perspectives in the program's implementation

One or two student representatives may also serve on the committee (in middle school grades or older). Alternatively, a separate student advisory group may be formed.

Committee and Staff Training
Before program implementation, members of the Bullying Prevention Coordinating Committee participate in a two-day training with a certified Olweus trainer. All other school personnel, including administrators, teachers, custodians, bus drivers, lunchroom and playground supervisors, support staff, and after-school program providers attend a one-day training. This training will give you a good understanding

of the program and provide the resources and support you will need to implement it successfully.

Schoolwide Implementation of the Olweus Bullying Questionnaire

Your help will be needed to administer the Olweus Bullying Questionnaire to your students before the program begins and at regular intervals after that. This anonymous questionnaire is designed for students in grades 3–12 and takes about 45 minutes to complete.

The Olweus Bullying Questionnaire serves three important purposes:

1. It creates awareness and involvement on the part of adults by providing detailed information about bullying and the social relationships among students.

2. It helps the school tailor its bullying prevention efforts to the needs of your particular school community.

3. It measures changes in bullying behavior over time and provides information on program progress and any bullying problems that need additional efforts.

The questionnaire results reveal the nature and extent of bullying at your school, including aspects of the school environment that might contribute to bullying. It will provide a common definition of bullying for students, and it will help your school plan for continued bullying prevention efforts and assess how the program is working over time.

You can also use the questionnaire results in your class meetings and discussions with students. Your Bullying Prevention Coordinating Committee will inform you of the schedule and procedures for administration. Typically, the questionnaire is administered every year, at the same time in the school year, and preferably no earlier than seven to eight weeks after your summer or winter vacations.

Your school's Bullying Prevention Coordinating Committee may hold a special meeting to review the results with staff. Be sure to attend this meeting, if held.

Staff Discussion Groups

Discussion groups for teachers and other school personnel involved in *OBPP* provide another level of support and information about the program and contribute to its success. The primary goals of staff discussion groups are

- to provide more detailed and comprehensive knowledge of *OBPP* and its various components

- to provide school staff with the opportunity to share ideas, ask questions, and practice solutions to various problem situations in a secure environment
- to stimulate faster implementation of the various components of the program
- to share experiences and viewpoints with others in similar situations and to learn from others' positive and negative experiences
- to create and maintain motivation and commitment
- to stimulate cooperation and coordination of program components and activities (to help develop a whole-school policy)

Each discussion group, of no more than fifteen people, meets regularly for approximately one hour, preferably every two weeks, but at least monthly for the first year of the program, and then somewhat less frequently after that.

These groups allow time for in-depth discussion about the program and reflection about the bullying prevention efforts at your school. As a teacher, you will find these discussions extremely helpful in solving problems and planning how to direct program activities in your classroom.

Introducing School Rules against Bullying
To ensure that students receive a consistent message throughout your school, every classroom will be asked to adopt the same four anti-bullying rules. Your school's Bullying Prevention Coordinating Committee may develop guidelines for consistent positive consequences for students who follow the rules and consistent negative consequences for students who break them. Although your school's committee may give you these consequences as general guidelines, how you apply them will vary somewhat depending on each bullying situation.

Reviewing and Refining the Supervisory System
One of the most important tasks of your school's Bullying Prevention Coordinating Committee will be to review and refine your school's supervisory system, so that bullying is less likely to happen. An important goal will be to use staff in effective ways to monitor and enforce anti-bullying rules throughout your school, and especially in "hot spots" like the playground/athletic fields, restrooms, and lunchroom.

Research in the United States, Norway, and other countries has shown that a large portion of bullying takes place during recess/breaks and on the playground. Research has also shown a link between "teacher (staff) density" during recess/breaks and the occurrence of bullying.[1]

Consequently, it is very important to have adequate adult supervision during recess/breaks and during other student activities. However, this is not just a question of numbers; the attitudes and actual behaviors of the supervising adults are clearly of utmost importance. A staff member who does not intervene in a bullying situation communicates to the students that bullying is okay and will not lead to any consequences for the perpetrators.

On the other hand, when supervising adults intervene firmly and consistently, this sends an important signal to the bullying students and possible bystanders: We don't accept bullying in our school, and such behavior will be stopped and/or negative consequences will be given.

In order for the supervisory system to function as well as possible, there must be coordination among the adults at school. The goal is to have staff reacting to bullying situations in reasonably consistent ways from one day or week to the next. Such coordination will result in a more effective supervisory system.

Another important part of a coordinated supervisory system is the exchange of information about what is happening during recess/breaks. Teachers who observe bullying or other undesirable behavior should, in addition to intervening, report their observations and any reactions or measures taken to the students' primary teachers, relevant homeroom teachers, or grade-level teams. The same procedure should be followed when observing students who often spend recess/breaks completely alone and who appear to be socially isolated.

Your school's Bullying Prevention Coordinating Committee may set up procedures whereby you will be asked to record the name and class of students involved in a bullying situation in a special log to be kept, for example, in the principal's office. This will increase the chances of discovering patterns in students' behavior or situations that may otherwise be easily overlooked. Check with your Bullying Prevention Coordinating Committee to see if such a log or other reporting system has been established.

There are a lot of teachers supervising the hallways and the outdoor commons area. Our school staff really does care about their students.

— A MIDDLE SCHOOL STUDENT

Duplicating this page is illegal. Do not duplicate without publisher's written permission.

41

You may be asked to monitor specific areas of your school outside of your classroom. Take this role seriously and intervene quickly and firmly when you spot a bullying problem. Chapter 8 will give you more information on how to do this.

Your school's Bullying Prevention Coordinating Committee also will be reviewing the design of your school to identify places where bullying can occur unseen by staff, and will be looking at ways to redesign supervision for these "hot spots" so that bullying is less likely to happen there.

School Kick-Off Event

Your school's Bullying Prevention Coordinating Committee will be planning an all-school kick-off event, using an assembly, skit, video, or group activity to introduce *OBPP* to students. This kick-off event will also introduce your school's anti-bullying rules and explain how bullying will be addressed throughout the school year. Plan to have your first class meeting shortly after this event to expand on the concepts and rules that were introduced.

Parent Involvement

Parents are important partners in addressing bullying. They are involved throughout the program by attending the kick-off event (optional), by coming to schoolwide parent meetings, and, whenever possible, by attending individual classroom parent meetings. One or more parents will also serve on the Bullying Prevention Coordinating Committee, providing input into the program and guidance on ways to keep parents informed of program events through letters, newsletters, or online bulletin boards. Of course, you will also be contacting parents as necessary to deal with bullying problems that occur in your classroom. Suggestions about how to make these interactions effective are provided in chapters 8 and 9.

Community Efforts

OBPP recommends working with the community to gain support for bullying prevention efforts in the school. Your school's Bullying Prevention Coordinating Committee will be involving community members such as volunteers or workers in youth organizations (e.g., youth recreation, scouting groups, sports clubs, or

**I really think our recess is more fun and better now because
I used to get glares and dirty looks—and all that has stopped. Thank you!**

— AN ELEMENTARY STUDENT

other youth clubs), city council members, county commissioners, and representatives from violence prevention coalitions, businesses, and faith-based organizations in your bullying prevention efforts.

Because students experience bullying both in and outside of school, it is also important to spread anti-bullying messages in other community settings where students gather. The committee will be encouraged to examine ways to spread anti-bullying messages beyond your school's doors through the media, local government, businesses, community nonprofit organizations, and law enforcement. Enlisting community support is another way to reinforce the message that bullying is not acceptable anywhere.

What Is the Usual Timeline for Implementing the Program?

Below is an optimal timeline for schoolwide implementation of *OBPP,* assuming a program launch at the beginning of the fall semester. (Alternatively, but somewhat less optimally, the program can be launched just after winter break, with the Olweus Bullying Questionnaire administered earlier in the fall and staff trainings held in the winter.)

Target Dates for Fall Launch	Activity
Late winter/early spring	Select members of the Bullying Prevention Coordinating Committee and an on-site OBPP coordinator.
March/April	Administer the Olweus Bullying Questionnaire.
April/May	Hold a two-day training with members of the Bullying Prevention Coordinating Committee.
May/June	Review data from the Olweus Bullying Questionnaire.
August/September	Conduct a one-day training with all school staff. Also hold your school kick-off event with students.
Beginning of the fall semester, following the one-day staff training	Plan, schedule, and launch other elements of the program: • Introduce school/class rules against bullying. • Begin class meetings. • Increase supervision; review and coordinate your supervisory system. • Initiate individual interventions with students. • Start regular staff discussion groups (scheduled before the school year starts). • Hold parent meetings.

Although this timeline provides a general framework for program implementation, it is important for each school to implement the program at its own pace and with integrity. Your school's certified Olweus trainer will help your Bullying Prevention Coordinating Committee consider a timeline that best fits your school's needs.

.   .   .

Getting Started
in the Classroom

WHAT YOU WILL LEARN IN CHAPTER 4	• the classroom components of *OBPP* • how to prepare for using *OBPP* in your classroom • other ways to promote *OBPP* in your classroom

The schoolwide components of *OBPP* were outlined in the last chapter. This chapter provides an overview of the program components that you will use to address bullying in your classroom. Most of these components are discussed in more detail in later chapters.

What Are the Classroom Components of *OBPP*?

Administration of the Olweus Bullying Questionnaire

As the last chapter noted, one of your first tasks with the program will be to administer the anonymous questionnaire to your students. Your Bullying Prevention Coordinating Committee will instruct you in how to do this.

Note: In some cases, the committee may have staff other than yourself administer the questionnaire to your students or may ask you to administer the questionnaire to students other than your own.

The questionnaire will be administered before the program begins and then again at regular intervals (usually annually at the same time of year). Because *OBPP* requires systemwide changes, changes in the level of bullying problems are not always seen right away. Many schools see significant changes immediately, but for some schools significant and lasting changes become visible after students have participated in the program for eight months or more.

You will need to make sure that students fill out the questionnaire completely and anonymously, so that your school's bullying information is as accurate as possible. If you have students in grades K–2 (the questionnaire is designed for students in grades 3–12), you will not administer the entire questionnaire, because the reading and conceptual levels are beyond that of most young students. However, if you would like to include younger students in this questionnaire process, talk with your Bullying Prevention Coordinating Committee and your certified Olweus trainer about developmentally appropriate ways to do this.

The questionnaire is also available in Spanish. Be sure to request Spanish copies if you have students in your classroom who would benefit from them.

The questionnaire will provide information about various aspects of bullying problems in your school. Many of the results can also be used as discussion-starters in your class meetings.

It should be noted, however, that the results of the questionnaire are not presented by classroom, but by grade and school level. This protects the identity of the students (who have been promised that their answers will be anonymous) and reduces the focus on possible problems in individual classrooms.

Generally, your Bullying Prevention Coordinating Committee will, in consultation with your school's certified Olweus trainer, arrange a staff meeting to present the survey results and to discuss how to interpret the results.

Discussion and Enforcement of Schoolwide Anti-Bullying Rules

You will want to introduce the schoolwide anti-bullying rules to your students. Post and discuss the rules in your class meetings so students have a clear understanding of what they are. Also discuss and use positive consequences for following the rules and the negative consequences for breaking them. Chapter 5 talks more about these anti-bullying rules and the use of positive and negative consequences.

RESEARCH FACT

An *OBPP* research study found that teachers who systematically implemented the anti-bullying rules in their classrooms experienced larger reductions in bullying problems one year after introduction of *OBPP*, compared to teachers who implemented the rules to a lesser degree or not at all. Similar results were obtained for the use of class meetings and role-playing, the two components of the program to be presented next.[1]

Class Meetings

Class meetings, together with class rules and role-playing, are among the most important components of *OBPP.* The purpose of these weekly (or more frequently, as you choose) meetings is to build a sense of class cohesion and community, to teach the rules and consequences of bullying, to help students understand their role in bullying situations, and to address issues about bullying as they arise.

Chapter 6 and resources on the Teacher Guide CD-ROM outline how to conduct these meetings and present a variety of meeting topics, guidelines for using role-plays in meetings, and suggestions for using the scenarios on the Teacher Guide DVD.

At first, your class meetings should focus on various aspects of bullying, but eventually you may want to use these meetings to address other more or less related topics.

Role-Playing

As a part of your class meetings, students will participate in role-playing. Role-plays help students problem-solve and generate solutions to bullying situations. They help students develop a repertoire of actions they can take when they are confronted with bullying situations. They also help students build empathy and perspective-taking skills by exploring the motivation and feelings of the characters in the scenarios.

Role-playing can be done in at least two different ways. You can have the students act out a bullying situation, or you can have them read about a situation or watch bullying scenarios on the Teacher Guide DVD. After either option, you will want to discuss the feelings and motives of the characters and then have students act out possible solutions. Guidelines on how to do either type of role-play effectively are provided in chapter 7.

Involving Parents

As chapter 3 mentioned, you are encouraged to hold parent meetings during the school year. These meetings help parents understand the issue of bullying, why the program is important, and the role they can play in its implementation. Additionally, having a strong partnership with parents in place will help if you need to call them later about their own child's involvement in bullying situations.

If parent meetings are a new concept to you, you may want to try holding grade-level parent meetings with other teachers at first. Once this relationship is established, you could then move to a classroom-level parent meeting.

Duplicating this page is illegal. Do not duplicate without publisher's written permission.

47

Parents are an integral part of any bullying prevention program. While your school's Bullying Prevention Coordinating Committee may plan formal ways of offering information to parents (for example, through workshops, newsletters, or special events), you will also be an important resource—informing parents of class meeting topics, encouraging them to become involved in your school's bullying prevention efforts, pointing them to helpful resources about bullying, and providing suggestions for follow-up activities at home with students who are bullied, students who bully, or students who are bystanders. More information about partnering with parents is presented in chapter 9.

It is also important to note that you will be involved in individual interventions with students who are bullied or who are bullying others, both in your classroom and throughout the school. More information on doing individual interventions is provided in chapter 8.

What Do You Need to Do to Get Ready to Implement *OBPP?*

Here are some tips that will help you prepare to implement the program in your classroom:

- Read this entire Teacher Guide and view the accompanying DVD.
- Review your notes and materials from the one-day *OBPP* training you attended (or will soon attend).
- Find out who your grade-level Bullying Prevention Coordinating Committee representative is and discuss any questions or suggestions you have with him or her.
- Attend staff discussion groups when they are set up at your school.
- Post the four anti-bullying rules in your classroom.

If, at first, you are not comfortable leading a class meeting (chapter 6), ask your school counselor, a Bullying Prevention Coordinating Committee member, or another teacher for assistance or advice. They may be able to model or co-lead your first session(s) with you.

You may also find it useful to do the following:

- Review other supplementary support materials that you could use in your classroom or with individual students and parents. (Additional resources are listed on the Teacher Guide CD-ROM.)
- Talk to your librarian about high-quality books and videos you can use in your classroom to initiate discussion about various aspects of bullying.

The Teacher Guide CD-ROM includes an *OBPP* Implementation Checklist that outlines the actions you should be taking in the classroom. It will be a helpful tool as you begin using the program. Your school's Bullying Prevention Coordinating Committee may also ask you to fill it out and turn it in. The actions described on this checklist will be described in more detail in later chapters of this guide.

The components we have described so far in this chapter are the most critical activities you can do in the classroom to reduce and/or prevent bullying. They should be implemented as consistently as possible to ensure positive results.

What Are Some Other Ways to Promote *OBPP* in the Classroom?

There are many ways to give *OBPP* a strong presence in your classroom. The following are some suggestions. These supplemental materials are enhancements to the program, not substitutes for class meetings and the other core components discussed earlier in this chapter. You may come up with other ideas as well. Be sure to share your ideas with other teachers and with your Bullying Prevention Coordinating Committee members.

Posters

The Teacher Guide CD-ROM includes PDF versions of two posters. Print out as many copies as you want, in whatever size you need. There is a poster high-lighting the four anti-bullying rules and a poster of suggested class meeting ground rules.

The posters are 8-1/2 x 11 inches, but can be enlarged as needed. They are available in both color and black and white on the CD-ROM. All posters are provided in English and Spanish.

You might also have your students make their own anti-bullying posters to display in your classroom or other school areas, such as the hallways, lunchroom, restrooms, or near your playground/athletic fields. Some schools have also printed the rules on large ripstop nylon banners that more permanently display the school rules against bullying.

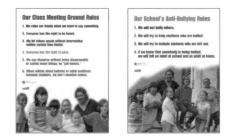

Duplicating this page is illegal. Do not duplicate without publisher's written permission.

49

Program Slogan

If your school has not developed a unique program slogan for your bullying prevention efforts, you may want to work with your students to come up with a slogan for your classroom. Here are some possible ideas:

- Our classroom is united against bullying!
- Care! Share! Be aware! Help stop bullying in our classroom!

The National Bullying Prevention Campaign, developed by the Health Resources and Services Administration, has the following slogan, which you may want to use:

- Take a stand. Lend a hand. Stop bullying now.

Encourage your students to create slogan posters, t-shirts, or other promotional materials.

Stickers

Have your students come up with sticker ideas that have an anti-bullying theme. Ideas include:

- Stop bullying
- the word "Bullying" in a circle with a line through it (for "No Bullying")
- Care!
- Lend a hand!

Give out the stickers as a reward to students who are following the four anti-bullying rules.

Table Tents

Table tents, available on the Teacher Guide CD-ROM, are tools for displaying your school's anti-bullying rules on classroom tables or on your desk. Print out a copy and fold it in half. Both English and Spanish language versions are available in color and black and white on the CD-ROM.

Schools around the country have found other creative ways to support the anti-bullying message. Some have designed pencils, notepads, student identification cards, and even school bags with an anti-bullying message. Be creative. Work with other teachers or your students on this, and see what you come up with for your classroom and school.

• • •

Setting Rules and Creating a Positive Classroom

WHAT YOU WILL LEARN IN CHAPTER 5	• the four anti-bullying rules and their meaning • appropriate positive and negative consequences to use with these rules • other strategies to create a positive classroom

One of the main objectives of *OBPP* is to create a safe and caring classroom environment that's free of bullying. An important way to achieve this is by introducing the four anti-bullying rules and applying positive and negative consequences to reinforce these rules.

What Should Be Your School Rules against Bullying?

Most likely your school already has some general rules regarding student conduct. It is very important, however, that your school also adopt rules specifically about bullying. *OBPP* recommends adopting four anti-bullying rules for the entire school and each classroom. These rules have been carefully developed to effectively address different aspects of bullying. For this reason, they should not be replaced or modified, except for minor word changes in rules 2–4.

Here are the four anti-bullying rules:

1. We will not bully others.

2. We will try to help students who are bullied.

3. We will try to include students who are left out.

4. If we know that somebody is being bullied, we will tell an adult at school and an adult at home.

RESEARCH FACT

> An *OBPP* research study has shown that teachers who systematically used these anti-bullying rules in their classrooms obtained larger reductions in bullying problems one year after introduction of *OBPP* compared to those who used the rules to a lesser degree or not at all.[1]

These rules cover both direct and more indirect forms of bullying, including social isolation and exclusion from the peer group (see the definition of bullying in chapter 2). Even though it is often a good strategy to word rules in a positive rather than a negative way (to emphasize what one can or should do rather than what one should not do), this is not a good idea with bullying. In *OBPP,* it is critical to communicate very clearly that bullying is not acceptable behavior. This is accomplished, among other ways, through the negatively worded rule 1. Rules 2–4 are worded more positively.

With every classroom in the school following the same rules, they are easier to enforce and students know more clearly what behavior is expected. This common set of rules sends a signal to students, parents, and others that your school has a unified and coordinated policy against bullying. These rules will be an independent part of your school's discipline policy.

RULE 1

We Will Not Bully Others

This is the most important anti-bullying rule. It sends a clear message to students that bullying is not acceptable in your classroom or school. Your responsibility, as

> There is a difference between ordinary classroom procedural rules such as raising your hand to talk, which are introduced to make your classroom activities run smoothly, and rules about bullying, which concern fundamental human rights.

a teacher, is to introduce the rule, make sure students understand what it means, and explain how the rule may be enforced. You can discuss the meaning of this and the other anti-bullying rules in several different ways, for example, in class meetings using role-plays or watching the Teacher Guide DVD scenarios.

How students and teachers relate to this rule depends to some extent on how the concept of bullying is defined and understood. In chapter 2, bullying is defined, discussed, and illustrated with examples.

In the majority of bullying situations, the students who are doing the bullying understand that what they are doing is negatively affecting the student who is being bullied, and they know they would not like to be treated this way themselves. Students who are bullying are also often eager to hide these activities from adults.

Even though there is a clear definition for bullying, in some situations it may be difficult to determine whether one is dealing with bullying or not. There are situations that represent a kind of "gray area" where different interpretations of the situation may come into play.

Those who are doing the bullying may claim, and perhaps also believe, that what they are doing is just a joke or "for fun." At the same time, the student who is being bullied may be quite troubled by the behavior. The use of nicknames is a common example: the person saddled with a nickname and the person using it may perceive the situation quite differently. Behavior that students who bully may call "teasing" is another example. How should such situations be handled?

Students who are being bullied are largely entitled to determine what constitutes undesirable behavior against them and what behavior they will and will not accept from others. Students who are subjected to something they do not like must have the right to express their disapproval of the behavior ("I don't like this") and expect that the other student(s) respect this feeling and stop the behavior.

Students who are subjected to bullying or other undesirable behaviors should be encouraged to express clearly to the student(s) displaying such behavior that they dislike the situation and do not want to be treated that way. Such clear expressions of disapproval may benefit these students in several ways:

- They learn to clarify what they are actually feeling and how they experience the behavior of others toward them. They put their own feelings and reactions into words.

- They gain power to define the limits of what behavior they will not take from others. Expressing their disapproval of a behavior will help them mark their "psychological territory."

- They learn to express their rights firmly and assertively, but not aggressively.

- They discover how to escape unpleasant and troublesome experiences (assuming that their expression of disapproval is respected). This can foster an increased sense of security and provide important experiences of coping and control.

When met with repeated, clear expressions of disapproval from the student who is bullied, students who bully or who are generally aggressive toward others may also learn some lessons:

- They may better understand how others perceive their behaviors. This may enable them to see things from another person's perspective.

- They may better understand that they must learn to respect others' feelings and reactions.
- They may clearly understand that what they may view as kidding, joking, or "fooling around" is often perceived in a much more negative way by those who are subjected to the behavior. With clear expressions of disapproval from a target, it will no longer be possible to believe or claim that "we're just playing" or that the whole thing is "just for fun."
- They may find it more difficult to continue with their negative activities without considering the reactions of others.

Although students need to clearly state when they don't approve of a behavior, it is not the student's responsibility to make the bullying stop. As with all interventions in this program, the adults in the school have a crucial role to play.

As the classroom teacher, you must assume the primary responsibility for introducing, clarifying, exercising, supervising, and enforcing the main rule 1, as well as the other anti-bullying rules.

The general anti-bullying rule 1 also applies to the adults at school. In-depth discussions on the meaning of this rule may serve as an important reminder that everyone in the school must be treated with respect.

RULE 2

We Will Try to Help Students Who Are Bullied

This rule stresses the importance of students taking a stand against bullying and siding with those who are being bullied. This attitude can be expressed in such behaviors as finding an adult to help intervene in a situation or actively defending the student who is being bullied (if this does not entail a risk of physical injury). It may also imply becoming a friend to the bullied student and clearly and openly refusing to participate in bullying behavior.

Through the Olweus Bullying Questionnaire, we found out that our kids wanted to help but weren't sure how to do so when someone was being bullied. The *Olweus Bullying Prevention Program* has given them the tools necessary to intervene, and they think it's cool to be known as a protector.

— ELEMENTARY SCHOOL COUNSELOR

Following this rule also can mean assisting or responding to the student who was bullied after the fact to provide comfort or social support. Exactly how particular students respond in any situation will depend on factors such as their age and size, gender, and social standing in their peer group.

Through discussions and role-plays you can help students develop a repertoire of appropriate actions to take in bullying situations and relationships. This rule reinforces the norm of caring for others that helps build a more positive community in the classroom.

RULE 3

We Will Try to Include Students Who Are Left Out

This rule is particularly designed for students who are exposed to indirect forms of bullying, such as intentional exclusion from the peer group. It is not uncommon to have one or more students in a classroom who are left out of most social activities.

The goal of this rule is that "everyone should have someone to be with." You can lead your students in a discussion about how to include classmates who are left out of activities, games, and group tasks in class, during the school day, and outside of school.

If you allow students to choose partners for special assignments or activities, be vigilant to potential problems. Bullied students often are repeatedly excluded from work groups. By assigning work groups yourself, you can ensure that no student will be excluded, and this may be a first step in ending this more subtle form of bullying.

Students can also benefit from a discussion about how to become more sensitive when inviting others to parties or social gatherings outside of school. Also help your students understand that sometimes students who have often been left out don't have much experience in being included. Or they might have been treated so badly by others that they are hesitant to join in, even when invited.

Including these students may take more than an invitation. It may also take patience and encouragement. It is important that you as the teacher recognize the efforts your students make to include others, even if those efforts are not initially successful.

RULE 4

If We Know That Somebody Is Being Bullied, We Will Tell an Adult at School and an Adult at Home

This rule emphasizes the importance of telling an adult if students know that someone is being bullied. It should be made very clear that rule 4 does not apply only to other students who are bullied. It also applies to situations where a student is being bullied himself or herself. This means, quite concretely: If I am bullied, I will tell an adult at school and an adult at home.

This rule is based on the fact that a considerable number, 30 to 60 percent, of students who are bullied do not tell an adult about it, neither at school or at home.[2] There may be several different reasons for this:

- They are afraid of retaliation from the students who bullied them and may even have been threatened with more bullying if they tell.
- They feel inadequate or ashamed for not being able to stop the bullying themselves.
- They feel that the bullying is their own fault and fear being blamed.
- They don't want to worry their parents and give them problems.
- They are afraid that their parents will cause trouble at school by overreacting.
- They are afraid that the situation may become worse if the teacher brings the problem up in the class.
- They may have previous experience that telling an adult does not solve the problem.

Even fewer students who witness bullying tell adults. Clearly, there is a great need for more open communication regarding bullying problems among students. Rule 4 has been created specifically to stimulate such communication. To some extent, this rule overlaps with rule 2—a natural way of helping students is to tell adults. However, rule 4 amplifies and extends beyond rule 2.

Your enforcement of the rules about bullying and the immediate action you take when confronted with information about a bullying situation will assure students that the problem will not go unnoticed if they tell an adult. It is extremely important that such information is taken seriously by the adults at school and is also followed up with investigations and intervention measures until the problem has been solved.

Students often do not tell adults about bullying because they see it, or are afraid that others will see it, as "tattling." Make sure your students understand that this is not tattling—it's simply following an anti-bullying rule that has been adopted by your school. To tell someone about bullying is thus something that is desired and prescribed by the adults at school. It is a very important prerequisite to creating a school environment with little or no bullying.

What Are Some Ways to Teach Students about the Four Anti-Bullying Rules?

It is possible to influence students' attitudes and behavior around bullying through discussions about the class rules. For example, your class could discuss passive participation in bullying. Some students rarely take the initiative to bully others, but "tag along" when another student leads the activity. It is important to make it clear that a student who passively participates has an individual responsibility for what happens. Outlines for classroom discussions of the rules are discussed in chapter 6.

Role-playing is also a very good strategy to initiate a discussion of the rules and a variety of bullying scenarios. For suggestions on role-playing, see chapter 7.

Another effective strategy to help clarify the rules is to read aloud excerpts from students' and young people's literature. However, choose material with care, as many stories are based on more or less incorrect perceptions of bullying.

It is important to be sure that all students in your classroom understand the four anti-bullying rules. Students will then gradually come to a common understanding of how the rules are to be interpreted, what is acceptable behavior, and what is unacceptable. This process may be particularly helpful for students who bully who are often not fully aware how much damage and suffering their behavior causes.

For the class rules to be effective—that is, to change student behavior and norms—they must be made clear. However, it is vital that the clarification be supplemented by other strategies as well. Some of these strategies concern your use of positive and negative consequences. Let's look at consequences now.

What Should Be the Consequences for Following or Not Following the Rules?

Note: Although these positive and negative consequences are discussed with regard to bullying behavior, they can be used for any antisocial or undesirable behaviors.

Positive Consequences

As you know, when students receive positive consequences for their behavior, they are more likely to behave the same way in similar situations in the future. In order for the anti-bullying rules to change behavior and norms, it is important that you, as the teacher, provide abundant positive reinforcement when students act according to the rules. You can give praise or use other positive consequences for the entire class, for a smaller group, or for individual students in recognition of behavior that conforms to the rules.

Types of Behavior to Reinforce

You could give positive reinforcement for the following types of actions:

- telling a student to stop teasing or kidding another student in a hurtful way
- taking the side of and supporting or defending a student who is being bullied
- letting the teacher know about a bullying situation that is occurring or a bullying relationship
- telling the teacher and parents when the student himself or herself is being bullied
- initiating activities that include all students in the class
- initiating activities that draw lonely students into activities with others
- being helpful and friendly to students who are often left out or made fun of

It is also important to reinforce actions not taken by certain students, for example, those who tend to be aggressive or who are easily influenced by others to join in on bullying. These students should be praised for *not* reacting aggressively in situations where they would normally do so, such as "Juan, you did a good job of keeping out of it when Jamal and Tyler were teasing Ben. You know that bullying is not allowed in our school."

Types of Positive Consequences

There are many ways to positively reward students in your classroom. You may already have a positive reinforcement system in place. Here are the major types of reinforcers:

- *Praise and friendly attention.* This includes verbal encouragement and recognition, smiles, nods, pats on the shoulder, and positive notes or phone calls home to parents. Praising students often and for specific behaviors can help create an environment of caring in your classroom.

- *Fun activities or privileges.* These include extra recess, choice time, watching a movie, class parties, or trips.
- *Healthy treats.* Give out healthy snacks such as fruit or popcorn.
- *Point systems.* Allow students to earn points that can be exchanged for prizes, special privileges, or activities or items that can be "purchased" with tickets.

Tips on the Use of Positive Consequences

- *Be specific.* It is important that students know exactly what they did to earn your praise so they can do it again. For example, "I really appreciate that you told me that Marcel was being bullied. I'm going to do something about that right away." A general "good job" can come off as insincere if given out too often.
- *Be quick.* Reinforce the behavior as soon as possible, preferably immediately after it occurs.
- *Do it often.* Reinforce often the positive things students are doing, especially when you are introducing something new, such as the rules against bullying. After the behavior has become more routine for students, decrease how often you reinforce it.
- *Be enthusiastic.* Show enthusiasm and warmth when you reinforce a behavior. Try to make eye contact with the student or students so they know that they have your undivided attention and that this is important to you.
- *Be consistent.* Try your best to react in similar ways to similar situations.
- *Be creative.* Try to use a variety of statements and methods of reinforcement. Using the same words all the time can begin to sound mechanical and insincere. When the desirable behavior is solidly in place, reinforcement needs to be given only now and then. Such partial reinforcement is particularly important for maintaining the desirable behavior.
- *Be honest.* Students can usually tell when the praise is not sincere.
- *Be in-the-know.* Find out what consequences are truly positive and culturally appropriate for individual students and your class. This is especially important for aggressive, antisocial students who often have a negative relationship to the school and to teachers. These students might not be very interested in verbal encouragement by the teacher. Look for unique consequences that will be attractive to them and may positively influence their behavior.

It's hard to keep track of how many positives and negatives you usually give to students. Ask a colleague to observe your teaching or record your teaching on video to see how you're doing in this area.

Negative Consequences

Unfortunately, positive reinforcement is not usually enough to get aggressive students to change their behavior. It is usually necessary to use negative consequences as well. When it comes to choosing a negative consequence, remember that negative consequences should be

- somewhat disagreeable or uncomfortable, but should not involve revenge or hostile punishment

- easy to use

- appropriate for the student's age, gender, and personality. Keep in mind that what seems a negative consequence to one student might not be for another. For example, a student who dislikes going out for recess may not find the revoking of recess privileges a negative consequence.

- logically related to the negative behavior of the student, if possible. For example, students who have broken or damaged another student's property may be required to replace it, fix it, or compensate for the loss in some way.

- aim at the undesirable behavior, not the person. Remember that students may do bad behaviors, but they should not be seen as bad people.

Types of Negative Consequences

Here are some examples of negative consequences:

- *Verbal rebukes or reprimands.* This is often the first kind of negative consequence that teachers use. For some students this is enough and for others it is not. Students who bully others may have received so much criticism or scolding over time that they don't react to verbal rebukes anymore. For these students a new twist may need to be added, such as a serious talk with the principal and/or parents/guardians, loss of privileges, or loss of recess for a specified period of time. Chapter 8 talks more about how to give effective verbal rebukes.

- *Time-outs.* By putting students in time-out, you take them away from other students or positive situations and place them somewhere that is less positive and interesting. This gives the students a chance to calm down while showing the rest of the class what the result will be of doing the same thing. Time-outs are usually used when a student continues to misbehave after verbal reprimands have been tried.

Time-outs should be

    a. used sparingly

    b. used only on students younger than twelve or thirteen years old

    c. fairly short, lasting five to fifteen minutes, depending on the age of the student and the circumstances involved

    d. carried out in a designated room or location in your classroom that is uninteresting, unattractive, and supervised

    e. explained clearly and matter-of-factly to the student. Name the specific reason for the time-out and the length of the time-out. This is not the time to have a discussion about what happened. You can discuss this with the student later. The goal of a time-out is to end the behavior and not to argue about it.

If the student refuses to go to the time-out, calmly give the student a choice to either go to the time-out now or add five more minutes to the time-out period. You can give the student a couple of minutes to make the decision.

It is important that the entire school staff agree on how and whether time-outs will be used. Check with your Bullying Prevention Coordinating Committee to see if time-out procedures have been established. You and all the other teachers will also need to explain this system to your students (and to parents) so students understand what they are to do when placed in time-out.

- *Response costs.* This means that a student loses a privilege or has to give up something positive that he or she expects to do or participate in, such as watching a movie or going on a field trip.

Here are some other possible negative consequences for students who break the classroom rule about bullying others:

- The student has to replace damaged clothing or property, preferably using his or her own money.

- The student who bullies others during lunch has to sit alone for a certain period of time.

- The student has to have a serious talk with you about what has happened and what is expected in the future.

Duplicating this page is illegal. Do not duplicate without publisher's written permission.

61

- The student has to stay close to you or another staff person who supervises recesses or breaks.
- You contact the student's parents to let them know about the inappropriate behavior.
- You set up meetings about the student's behavior with the principal or assistant principal.
- Parents are required to come to the school to discuss their child's behavior. If the bullying or other negative behavior is serious, parents may also be required to come immediately to the school and remove the child from the school for some (short) period.

In very serious cases of bullying, administrators may want to consider suspending the student from school for the remainder of the day in order to emphasize the significance of the bullying. Suspensions should be used very judiciously, however. Lengthy suspensions for bullying are not recommended. A student who is bullying others needs to learn how to interact with students in a more positive way. By removing students from school, they lose the opportunity to learn this.

Discussing Negative Consequences as a Class
When you discuss the four anti-bullying rules, also discuss the consequences of breaking rule 1: We do not bully others. Have students suggest possible consequences for breaking this rule. Some students may suggest consequences that are more severe than you would use; regardless, holding this discussion is likely to make the consequences seem fairer to the students when implemented.

Having this discussion may be particularly important for aggressive students who tend to feel singled out and treated unfairly by teachers. Such reactions are less likely to occur if the entire class discussed the necessity of having consequences for undesirable behavior.

Another benefit of discussing the consequences with your class is that it helps those who bully others to see that most students find bullying unacceptable. Again, this reinforces an anti-bullying norm in your classroom and school. Students who might be more inclined to bully others will feel peer pressure not to do so.

And, as has already been mentioned, it is important to be aware of your own behavior and interactions with students and adults at school. It is possible for teachers to bully students and take advantage of the power they have over them. You are an important role model and, no matter what you are doing, you are always teaching by your example.

Besides implementing the four anti-bullying rules, it is also helpful to think about your classroom-management practices, to see if there is anything you can do to help foster a more positive, caring classroom community.

What Are Some Ways to Create Positive Classroom Management?

There are many attitudes and actions that make up positive classroom management. Following is a sample of some of them. Take a few minutes to read through this list and check off which ones you already have in place and which ones you might want to work on as you begin using *OBPP*.

It may be helpful to ask a colleague to rate you on this checklist as well. Another teacher's perspective might reveal additional areas of strength and areas of potential growth. Most of us will benefit from this type of review on a regular basis.

As mentioned in chapter 3, *OBPP* is not a classroom-management technique, although many of the principles of good classroom management are clearly compatible with the principles of *OBPP*. Good classroom management is likely to facilitate good and effective implementation of *OBPP*, however.

GOT IT! NEEDS WORK

☐ ☐ *Positive expectations of students.* You make it clear to students that you expect each person can and will learn, to the best of his or her abilities, and behave appropriately.

☐ ☐ *Caring attitude.* You project an attitude of caring, involvement, and respect by the way you treat your students, by the tone of voice you use when speaking with them, and by your efforts to get to know them personally.

☐ ☐ *Students have potential for success.* You measure progress and success according to the abilities of each student. You help students work at their own level so they don't get frustrated or feel like failures.

☐ ☐ *Classroom climate of cooperation.* You set expectations and provide opportunities for students to help each other, work in cooperative groups, and encourage each other to do their best.

☐ ☐ *Positive group identity.* Your class has the opportunity to get to know each other, have fun together, and feel successful as a group. This might be through games, projects, or reaching classroom goals.

GOT IT! NEEDS WORK

☐   ☐   *Students know what to expect from you.* As you know, students place a high value on fairness. You mix praise and positive reinforcement with setting limits, rules, and enforcing consequences so students know what is expected of them and what to expect from you.

☐   ☐   *Students are given responsibilities in the classroom.* Students are given responsibilities or jobs such as helping another student, leading a class meeting or discussion, or taking attendance. Trusting them with these responsibilities gives them a sense of belonging and also affects their relationship with you in a positive way.

☐   ☐   *Classroom procedural rules.* You and your students create classroom procedural rules or ground rules that keep the classroom a learner-friendly environment. You take time at the beginning of the year to create these rules, maybe using role-plays or classroom discussions to make sure students understand what the rules mean. These are ordinary class rules, such as raising your hand to speak, that are used in addition to the four anti-bullying rules.

☐   ☐   *Consistent follow-up and enforcement of the rules.* You make sure students understand the consequences for breaking the rules, and you consistently and fairly carry out these consequences when the rules are broken.

☐   ☐   *Preparedness and organization.* You have a clear plan about what you are doing each day. You are prepared and organized. Of course, there are days when things just don't go the way you want them to, but being organized allows little chance for students to get off task or become distracted. Students also know the goal of the lessons you are teaching and what is expected of them.

☐   ☐   *With-it-ness.* You have a continuous awareness of what is happening in all parts of the classroom. Students know you as "having eyes in the back of your head."

☐   ☐   *Your focus in the classroom.* Most of the time, you have a "group focus," addressing all students in the class and holding their attention for significant periods of time. However, you are also able to switch quickly between a group focus and a focus on individual students.

GOT IT!   NEEDS WORK

☐   ☐   *Appropriate pacing.* Teachers are often expected to juggle many things at once in the classroom. You are able to handle multiple tasks and maintain a teaching pace that meets the needs of all students as much as possible.

☐   ☐   *Variety in teaching styles.* You use many different ways to present a lesson. Using different teaching methods throughout the day helps you and your students stay interested and engaged.

☐   ☐   *Smooth transitions.* Transitions can often lead to opportunities for disruptive behavior, including bullying. By planning transitions or having a repertoire to choose from easily, you maintain order in the classroom when moving from one activity to the next.

☐   ☐   *Cooperation with parents.* You establish strong relationships with your students' parents and see them as part of a team whose goal it is to make school a successful and positive experience for their children.

.   .   .

6

Holding Class Meetings

WHAT YOU WILL LEARN IN CHAPTER 6	• the purposes of class meetings • what should be discussed in the first few class meetings • what additional topics can be addressed through class meetings

In the last chapter you learned about the classroom and school rules against bullying and how to create a positive classroom climate. Holding regular class meetings will help your students understand what the rules mean and how they play out in their daily school lives. Begin facilitating weekly class meetings shortly after the schoolwide kick-off event. Class meetings are a key component of *OBPP*.

This chapter describes how to organize class meetings and provides suggested topics for these discussions.

RESEARCH FACT

An *OBPP* research study has shown that teachers who systematically used class meetings in their anti-bullying work obtained larger reductions in bullying problems one year after introduction of *OBPP* compared to those who used class meetings to a lesser degree or not at all.[1]

IMPLEMENTATION TIP

If you already use class meetings as part of your classroom routine or as part of another program, maintain the structure you've been using but focus your discussions on bullying and related issues.

What Are the Purposes of Class Meetings?

Class meetings are designed

- to teach students what bullying is, the meaning of the four anti-bullying rules, and different ways of reacting when bullying occurs; and to build a commitment among students to follow these rules

- to help students learn more about themselves and their feelings and reactions, and those of their peers, and to provide them with opportunities to express their personal opinions in a relatively safe and supportive environment

- to build a sense of community and belonging and to help develop a set of norms about bullying and other important issues that is shared by a majority of the students in the class

- to help you, as the teacher, learn more about the classroom culture, power struggles, and relationships among classmates, and what goes on in the group (the "inner life" of the class). This will help you identify bullying relationships and discover bullying tendencies at an early stage before problems fully develop.

- to provide a forum for dealing with bullying problems in the classroom and, more generally, for the discussion and possible solution of other problems in the classroom

- to provide a forum for discussing and following up on decisions regarding individual interventions (discussed in chapter 8)

Class meetings are not the same as curriculum lessons. Although you have information you will want to share with students, a class meeting is designed to establish communication among all members of your class. You will want to provide time for students to share their opinions and allow students to guide the discussion when it is appropriate.

Teachers vary in their experience and comfort level with class meetings. There is no one right way to lead a class meeting. Some teachers prefer to have a very clear idea of what is going to be discussed, so we have provided several outlines

Class meetings have really helped with outside recess. Kids are really following the rules and treating each other with more respect.

— AN ELEMENTARY STUDENT

and scripts on the Teacher Guide CD-ROM. Other teachers desire a more open-ended style that provides flexibility to discuss issues as they come up. Either approach is fine.

If you don't feel comfortable leading these meetings at first, ask for help from your Bullying Prevention Coordinating Committee members. Perhaps one of them could lead the first couple of meetings for you or you could co-lead the meetings. Or consider asking another teacher with experience in class meetings to co-facilitate with you. Your Bullying Prevention Coordinating Committee may also offer additional training on conducting class meetings, and you may want to raise issues about these meetings at your staff discussion group.

What Steps Should Be Taken to Organize and Lead Class Meetings?

Your role in leading class meetings is more of a facilitator than teacher. This does not mean you will not guide the discussion. You will need to make sure your discussion goals are met through the careful use of probing and open-ended questioning. Class meetings are an opportunity for students to share their feelings and opinions, and to suggest solutions, as they learn about how to follow the rules, interact as a community, and handle bullying situations appropriately.

When planning and leading your class meetings, keep the following in mind:

- It works best to have students sit in a circle or half circle. This allows for more intimate interactions and eye contact among students. If age-appropriate for your students and if time is a concern, practice the process of getting into a circle before you start having class meetings. This may mean moving chairs or pushing desks to the side. You may want to challenge the class to get safely and quietly into a circle within a certain period of time, say, one minute.

- Class meetings should be held regularly, preferably at least once a week. For upper primary and middle or junior high students, the meetings could last 30 to 40 minutes. Meetings for younger students could last 15 to 30 minutes. With younger students, you may want to have more than one meeting per week.

- It works best to have the meetings at a specific time, preferably at the end of the week so you can talk about how the week went and make plans for the next week. Friday meetings work well, but not the last period of the day. You might need to occasionally reschedule your meeting if something comes up that needs immediate attention during your regularly scheduled time.

- You are the leader or facilitator of the group. If you feel a second leader is necessary for small-group discussions or because of certain classroom conditions, ask another teacher, counselor, or mental health professional to help you, but do not turn over your class meetings entirely to another person.

  Work with the students to develop some basic ground rules for your class meetings from the very beginning. Here are some sample rules:

  1. We raise our hands when we want to say something.
  2. Everyone has the right to be heard.
  3. We let others speak without interrupting (within certain time limits).
  4. Everyone has the right to pass.
  5. We can disagree without being disagreeable or saying mean things; no "put-downs."
  6. When talking about bullying or other problems between students; we don't mention names.

     However, it is important that students tell you or another adult (rule 4) if they know or suspect a bullying problem in the classroom. When this rule is presented, you may want to tell the students: "If you know of someone who is being bullied or is bullying others, please come talk to me after our class meeting or sometime later."

  Note: There is a class meeting ground rules poster on the Teacher Guide CD-ROM in both English and Spanish (see page 49).

- You might want to switch from large-group discussions to small-group discussions from time to time or within the same meeting. You could start off with one type of grouping and end in the other. This adds variety to the meetings and provides an opportunity for students who feel more at ease speaking up in a small group to do so.

- Sometimes it is a good idea to have students consider a topic individually and write down their thoughts and suggestions before they enter into a group discussion. Writing such short essays can be used as a pre-meeting activity that allows students to think more deeply about the subject before discussing it. Reflecting on the topic or question individually also helps students form their own opinions before they hear those of other students who might influence them.

- Don't allow students to intimidate others during the meetings. Take the lead in reinforcing the message that all bullying incidents will be addressed.

Also stress that if you hear about any retaliation for what is said by students during a class meeting or to you afterward individually, there will be consequences for this as well.

- Sometimes you may want to bring up a specific bullying problem in your classroom, but this should be done only if all students involved have given you permission to do so. In these cases, names may be used, but be sure to manage this situation and the resulting discussion so that all students are respected and the focus is on positive solutions.

- Be aware that you will likely have students who are being bullied by others in your group. Do not force students to talk about their experiences unless they feel comfortable doing so and unless you feel prepared to facilitate this discussion. Be sensitive to the painfulness of bullying and the tremendous impact it can have on students. Do not make light of bullying situations and do not allow other students to do so either.

- Here are some things to remember about your role as the discussion leader:

  1. Be an attentive listener, and even though you might have to correct or remind a student who is out of line, you should not be derogatory.

  2. You are responsible for making sure the viewpoints of all students are heard, including students who are shy or hesitant to speak in a group. You might need to address these students directly, such as, "Now I am interested in hearing what Emily thinks." You could also go around the circle to get opinions from all students, allowing students to "pass" if they're not yet comfortable speaking.

  3. There are often students who tend to dominate the conversation. You will have to monitor this and possibly interrupt these students by saying something like, "Mario, thanks for sharing your thoughts, but hold off for just a moment. I would like to hear what Brianna thinks first," Or, "I've noticed that a few are doing most of the talking. Let's hear from someone who's not spoken yet."

  4. When students try to interrupt, remind them of the ground rules that were set up at the beginning of your class meetings.

- It is important to keep your class meetings fresh and interesting for students. While it is desirable to revisit *OBPP* themes and concepts, vary your approach. For example, some meetings could be teacher-directed. Some meeting topics could be initiated by students. Some meetings could have

Duplicating this page is illegal. Do not duplicate without publisher's written permission.

71

planned themes, while others are more open-ended, responding to the needs at hand. Some meetings should focus on bullying, while others should address additional topics of interest. You can also vary the activities and methods used, such as using student literature, audiovisual materials, group or pairs work, role-playing, and making connections between *OBPP* themes and academic themes being taught in your classroom.

What Should You Discuss in Your Class Meetings?

Here is a suggested sequence for your initial class meetings on bullying:

- Introduce the concept of class meetings and define bullying. Print out the First Class Meeting Outline and Script from the Teacher Guide CD-ROM. (Suggested time: At least one class meeting.)

- Discuss what the four anti-bullying rules are and what these rules mean in concrete terms. Use lots of examples to illustrate and clarify the meaning of the rules and their possible implications. Students should be able to recite these rules from memory and understand how they are applied. Use the outlines and scripts on the Teacher Guide CD-ROM. Reinforce the rules by playing Bullying Rules Roundup, found in both English and Spanish on the Teacher Guide CD-ROM. This game gives students practice in remembering the rules and applying them in bullying situations. (Suggested time: Four to five class meetings.)

- Discuss how bullying affects the student who is bullied and what the characteristics are of students who bully others. Give examples of bullying situations or play scenarios on the Teacher Guide DVD to help students think about how it would feel to be bullied and what might be the consequences for the student who does the bullying. Video scenario discussion questions are provided on the Teacher Guide CD-ROM. (Suggested time: One to two class meetings.)

- Use information from the introduction and chapter 2 of this guide to talk about short-term and long-term consequences of bullying. (Suggested time: One class meeting.)

We have our class meetings every Thursday, and they are fun.

It has changed our school quite a bit.

— A MIDDLE SCHOOL STUDENT

- Discuss what can be done if we know a student is being bullied. Play scenarios from the Teacher Guide DVD and have students come up with suggestions for what adults, the bullied student, and other students can do. (Suggested time: One to two class meetings.)

- Discuss what roles students play in bullying situations. Use the Bullying Circle to explain how all students are involved in bullying even if they don't do anything. A reproducible copy of the Bullying Circle is also available on the CD-ROM. Also consider doing the Bullying Circle Exercise available on the CD-ROM. Then talk about how students can be involved in a more positive way. You can use role-plays or play scenarios from the Teacher Guide DVD to help students understand this better. Scenarios 2, 3, and 5 have been specifically designed to show the various roles in the Bullying Circle. (Suggested time: Two to three class meetings.)

- Discuss these questions: What if we bully others? How can we recognize and change our behavior so that we aren't bullying others (either actively or passively by encouraging others to bully)? (Suggested time: One class meeting.)

- Discuss what a positive classroom is like, and what does and does not happen in a positive classroom. Have students come up with ways to improve their classroom environment to make it more positive. (Suggested time: One to three class meetings.)

After some of these topics have been covered, other class meetings can be used to follow up on how students are using the rules or to talk about specific kinds of bullying problems at your school or common locations where bullying is taking place.

Discussions about how students have followed or not followed the four anti-bullying rules can put social pressure on students who tend to bully others. They will see that most of their classmates don't like bullying, and this may influence their behavior in a more positive way.

Although your class meetings will initially focus on the topic of bullying, these meetings can be used for other topics as well. Students may become bored if bullying and associated problems are the only topics discussed. After a number of class meetings with a main focus on bullying, you can use these meetings as a forum to deal with any classroom issues, to build class cohesiveness and community, and to recognize achievements and successes of the class.

Duplicating this page is illegal. Do not duplicate without publisher's written permission.

73

However, the topic of bullying and the current state of bullying in your classroom should be talked about again and again with some regularity.

Here is a list of additional topics that can be used in class meetings. Also discuss these topics with other teachers at your grade level to see if there are ways to weave these topics into your regular curriculum or use of literature.

Additional Class Meeting Topics

1. Team building among students
2. Gender issues in bullying (differences between boys and girls)
3. Cyber-bullying (see page 28)
4. Bus behavior
5. Playground behavior
6. Cafeteria behavior
7. Nonverbal communication
8. Listening skills
9. Other communication skills
10. Current events, particularly as they relate to bullying and school safety
11. Bullying-related literature, after it has been read aloud or silently in class
12. Identifying feelings
13. Friendship
14. Peer pressure
15. Assertive versus aggressive behavior
16. Diversity
17. Prejudice
18. Respect
19. Trust
20. Regular check-ins to see how your classroom community is doing

Kids love to share stories, and class meetings give them the opportunity to share while conveying an anti-bullying message.

— PREVENTION SPECIALIST

21. Planning a recreational event together

22. Guest speaker with a follow-up classroom discussion

23. Anger and healthy ways to handle it

24. Empathy for others

25. Problem-solving

26. Courage

27. Popularity

28. How your class can influence others in a positive way

29. Student suggestions, from an anonymous suggestion box set up in the classroom

How Can You Evaluate the Progress of Your Class Meetings?

Evaluating your class meetings will help to refine them and improve their effectiveness. Remember, if you have never facilitated this type of meeting before, it may take a few attempts before these meetings run smoothly. A Class Meeting Activity Log has been useful for many teachers in evaluating their meetings. It also reminds you of what has been said and done in previous class meetings and helps you plan for the future. A copy is available on the Teacher Guide CD-ROM.

. . .

We need to do the right thing when we see bullying happening.
We learned what to do in our class meetings, and
we practice what we are shown to do.

— STUDENT

Using Role-Plays

WHAT YOU WILL LEARN IN CHAPTER 7	• the benefits of using role-plays in class meetings • guidelines for using role-plays • how to conduct role-plays with solutions and without solutions

In the last chapter you learned about how to run class meetings. Some of your class meetings will involve role-play activities. This chapter provides guidance in how to use role-playing.

RESEARCH FACT

An *OBPP* research study has shown that teachers who systematically used role-playing in their anti-bullying work obtained larger reductions in bullying problems one year after introduction of *OBPP* compared to those who used role-playing to a lesser degree or not at all.[1]

What Are the Benefits of Using Role-Plays?

Role-playing

- gives students insight into the different types of bullying and what roles bystanders, followers, and defenders might take in each situation
- helps students develop a better emotional understanding of how the different participants feel in bullying situations and what motivates them to do what they do
- provides a great springboard for discussions about bullying and ways to stop it

- provides valuable opportunities for students to practice, test, and evaluate solutions to bullying situations. When students act out these behaviors, they also model them for others. It can be especially powerful for students to see social leaders in the classroom modeling behavior that rejects bullying or intervenes in a bullying situation.

IMPLEMENTATION TIP

Role-playing usually works best with students in grades 4 or higher. If you are working with a younger age group, you may need to describe the scenarios rather than use the scripts provided, or help act out the scene with the students.

What Kinds of Role-Playing Are There?

There are at least two effective types of role-playing that you can use with your students:

Role-Playing without Solutions

The main goal in this type of role-play is for students to gain a good understanding of the feelings and motivations of the characters involved in a bullying situation. Try this type of role-play first. Understanding the emotional aspects of bullying helps students see the need to intervene and builds empathy. If your students immediately try to find solutions, they might overlook this important step. Role-playing without solutions and the discussion that follows should focus on the motivations and feelings of the characters involved and not on what should be done about the bullying.

Role-Playing with Solutions

The important goals of this type of role-play are to give students an opportunity to arrive at, test, and evaluate solutions to bullying situations. This type of role-play helps students develop a repertoire of tools they can use to address a bullying situation, whether they are themselves being bullied or are bystanders.

Should Students Be Allowed to Act Out Bullying Situations?

Before using role-plays, you will need to answer an important question for yourself: Are you comfortable allowing students to act out bullying situations, or would you prefer students role-play only solutions? Some educators fear that allowing students to actually mimic acts of bullying may increase the risk of bullying behavior.

If you are comfortable having students act out bullying situations, sample scripts are provided in both English and Spanish on the Teacher Guide CD-ROM in the Role-Play Activities document. Using these scripts helps you manage student interactions. We encourage you to begin by having students closely follow the scripts. Once you and the students are comfortable with the use of role-plays, you might then encourage them to develop scenarios of their own.

If you are uncomfortable having students act out bullying situations, we suggest that you have students watch one of the bullying scenarios on the Teacher Guide DVD. Then students can role-play positive solutions to the bullying situation. Discussion questions for each video scenario are provided on the Teacher Guide CD-ROM (see page 72). Another option is to begin reading a story about bullying and stop the story so students can act out a positive ending.

Although the choice is up to you and your school's Bullying Prevention Coordinating Committee, we encourage teachers to consider using role-plays that act out bullying situations for the following reasons:

- Since you will be having a strong anti-bullying message in your classroom, most students are likely to see the bullying as wrong, even if they portray characters who are involved in bullying others.

- You will be able to control who plays the role of the student(s) who bully and the student who is bullied, thereby avoiding some problematic assigning of roles.

- The role-plays provided in this guide are common bullying situations. It is unlikely that they will give students any new ideas of how to bully others.

- Most students will have seen more extreme cases of bullying or violence in the media, and perhaps in your school.

- We are unaware of any research that has shown that acting out bullying behaviors actually promotes those behaviors in real life. Role-playing these behaviors in a controlled environment and discussing the motivations and feelings of the characters involved may actually be a strong learning experience, helping students understand the perspective of those who are bullied.

Certainly having students role-play bullying situations may allow some difficult interactions to arise, but the following guidelines will help you to avoid many of these issues. Go over these guidelines with students *before* they act out bullying situations.

- Initially, stress with students the importance of following the script as written and not adding anything to the script.

Duplicating this page is illegal. Do not duplicate without publisher's written permission.

79

- No one in the role-play should be physically hit or pushed; the students should only pretend to do these actions or stop the role-play before it gets to that point.

- No inappropriate words may be used, such as swear words or derogatory nicknames. Remind students that words can carry much weight and be very hurtful.

- The students should take the bullying situation seriously. Don't allow students to use this type of role-play as an opportunity to make fun of students who are bullied or make light of those who bully others.

- As will be discussed later, help students get out of their roles after the role-play is done.

- Be sure to allow ample time for serious discussion at the end of each role-play. During this discussion, anti-bullying messages can be strongly communicated.

What Should You Do Before You Use Role-Playing in Your Class Meetings?

1. Read through the two role-play situations from the Role-Play Activities document and choose one for the students to use during a class meeting.

2. Decide how you will divide your students into groups. You may already have established cooperative learning groups in your classroom and may wish to use those groupings. If you want to use role-plays where the characters are all girls or all boys, adjust the groups accordingly.

   As you work on these scenarios, you may find that your groups have more students than character parts. If so, assign the other students roles as observers or bystanders. Another alternative is to have each group perform the role-play several times with different players so that everyone has an opportunity to play a role.

   All students should participate in the discussion before and after the role-play. The role-plays without solutions don't take much time. It is the discussions that occur before and after the role-play that may be most important.

3. If an obvious bullying problem does not exist in your classroom and none of your students are socially isolated (and at increased risk of being subjected to bullying), you may choose to let the students decide who will play each role. If, on the other hand, you know or suspect that a student is likely to be

bullied or there are students who tend to bully others in your classroom, then you should use the following guidelines in assigning parts:

IMPLEMENTATION TIP

If you're uncertain whether or not there are problems of bullying/social isolation in your classroom, err on the side of safety and assign parts.

- Students with bullying tendencies should usually not play bullying roles. Instead, give these students the role of the student who is bullied so they can experience what this feels like. Or assign them to be part of a group of students who feels that the bullying is wrong and intervenes. Playing such roles may help these students see that many others in your classroom do not approve of bullying. Another alternative is to give these students, possibly together with others, the task of defending the vulnerable student.

- Students who are subjected to bullying in any form should not be assigned the role of the student who is bullied. This role could be very stressful for them. (An exception might be if the student asks to play this role and seems strong enough for it.) Students who appear to be more vulnerable should probably also not play the role of a student who bullies, so the other students do not feel that retaliating is a solution to bullying. It may be best for these students to be part of the group of bystanders that intervenes in the situation.

  It is important to think about these aspects of the role-plays; however, as the teacher, you should use your own discretion when assigning parts. You know your students best and might feel that it would be helpful for certain students to play certain roles.

  For example, some students who have shown bullying tendencies suddenly become aware of their own behavior and their friends' reactions when they play the role of a student who bullies. Such insight could prompt these students to change their behavior. It is not easy to predict how different students will respond to different roles.

4. Decide how you will have the students perform their role-plays. Some students may feel anxious or nervous about performing in front of the class. You might want to start with some warm-up exercises, such as having the class play a game of charades or share personal stories with the rest of the

Duplicating this page is illegal. Do not duplicate without publisher's written permission.

81

class to create a more relaxed, less critical atmosphere. Or break the class into two small groups to act out the role-plays, instead of performing for the whole class.

After the small-group performances, you could ask for volunteer groups to do the role-play in front of the whole class. This way there will be a role-play or role-plays that everyone in the class has seen and can discuss.

5. Watch the group dynamics in the role-play situations very carefully. At the end of the role-play, help "take students out of their roles" before dismissing them from the role-play to go back to their seats. You can do this through asking questions of the actors, such as

- What did you like or dislike about how your character behaved?

- What would you have done differently in this situation?

- What was realistic or not realistic about this role-play?

How Do You Use Role-Plays without a Solution?

Here are the basic steps you should take in doing role-plays without solutions. Again, this type of role-play is meant to help students understand the emotional consequences of bullying. A key part of this type of role-play is the discussion that occurs afterward.

These steps outline role-plays where students act out bullying situations.

1. Explain to students that they will be doing some role-plays. If you have not done role-plays in your classroom before, explain that a role-play is like acting out a situation that could really happen. Also explain that being in a role-play or watching one helps you think about what it might feel like to actually be in that situation so you can figure out what to do.

2. Divide the class into small groups and give each group a bullying scenario script and a copy of the Character Sketch Worksheet (available in the Role-Play Activities document on the Teacher Guide CD-ROM). Either assign parts or allow students to assign parts. These materials are available in both English and Spanish.

3. Have students read through the script together and then work as a group on a character sketch for each character in the role-play. This may take 15 to 20 minutes to do. Students should use the worksheet as a guide in their discussions. This will help them understand their characters better. After they have completed the character sketches, they should practice the role-play again and think about any props they might need.

82

4. Remind students about the Bullying Circle and how everyone in a bullying situation has a role to play. You might want to have the Bullying Circle diagram available for students to refer to while they work on their role-plays. A copy of the Bullying Circle diagram is on the Teacher Guide CD-ROM (see page 73).

5. Give each group a reasonable amount of time to work on their role-play and the character sketches (15 to 20 minutes for discussion and 10 to 15 minutes to practice acting out the scenarios). Encourage students to be creative and to really try to understand their characters in the scenario, what they are thinking, and why they do what they do.

6. When the students have completed their character sketches and have finished practicing their role-play, call the students together. Briefly remind them what appropriate audience behavior is expected in your classroom (such as no interrupting, no laughing, no side conversations).

7. Call on each group to present their role-play to the class (or to each other in smaller groups and then the class as was mentioned earlier). Unless there is a fight or an argument, you should not intervene in the role-plays.

8. After each role-play, thank the students for their efforts. If the situation was not clear in the role-play, briefly discuss what took place.

9. After the role-plays are finished, lead the class in a follow-up discussion. This is the most important part of the role-playing activity.

The Follow-Up Discussion

When discussing role-plays without a solution, focus on the emotional and psychological aspects of the scenario. Rather than discussing solutions, guide students in talking about the actions, reactions, and relationships of the characters. The goal of the discussion is for students to gain a better understanding of possible causes and effects of bullying on all students involved. Ideally, the discussion will result in the majority of students feeling empathy and compassion for the student who is bullied and a negative attitude toward bullying behavior.

Remind students that they should try to think about how these characters felt and acted, rather than how they personally feel about the situation. This approach helps students express their personal feelings in a safe way, especially if they feel uncomfortable talking about their own feelings.

To begin with, they should try to answer the questions from the perspective of the characters. You could say: "Now I want you to try to forget about yourselves.

Duplicating this page is illegal. Do not duplicate without publisher's written permission.

83

Think first about the characters you have played (or observed). When we ask questions, you can tell us what you think these characters are thinking and feeling. What kind of people are they, and how did they get to be the way they are?"

First ask the questions to the actors about their individual roles, and then open up the discussion to the entire class. You will find suggested questions below. Start the discussion by asking the student who played the student who was bullied about his or her character, followed by the bystanders and then the student or students who were bullying others. Use the appropriate characters' names in asking these questions:

1. What was the bullied character thinking, and what did it feel like when he or she was bullied?

2. Why do you think this character was bullied? (Be certain to correct students if they begin to blame the student who was bullied.)

3. Why do you think the other students joined in the bullying?

4. What do you think the other characters were thinking?

5. What do you think the bullying character is like?

6. Why does he or she treat the other student this way?

After this discussion, you could ask students to come up with solutions and then act them out to see which ones would be the most successful and why. This next section will give you guidance on how to do this.

How Do You Use Role-Plays with Suggested Solutions?

Note: Depending on the time you have available, you may want to use these role-plays in a later class meeting after covering the same role-plays without solutions.

After doing role-plays without suggested solutions, it's important to follow up with role-plays with suggested solutions. These provide students with opportunities to arrive at, test, practice, and evaluate appropriate solutions to bullying situations.

These steps outline role-plays with suggested solutions:

1. Divide the class into the same small groups that they were in when they did the role-plays without solutions.

2. Explain that they will be acting out the same role-plays as before but will be picking up where the action left off last time and will be working on possible solutions to the situation. They will be answering the questions What will happen next? How can there be a positive solution to the situation? Remind students that the best solution may be to seek help from adults.

3. Give each group their script (same as the earlier script) and a Role-Play Solutions Worksheet, also in the Role-Play Activities document available on the Teacher Guide CD-ROM.

4. Tell the class that they will now work together to come up with possible solutions to the situations they acted out. They should first read the role-play again and then work on developing several possible solutions. These solutions must be realistic, meaning they could really happen and without extraordinary financial or technical help.

   Solutions should also be clear and not too complicated, and they should not involve any violence or retribution toward the student(s) who bullied others. If students create unrealistic solutions, you and the rest of the students can gently point out how ineffective or problematic these choices may be and why.

   Solutions can involve people not mentioned in the scenario, such as teachers, parents, or principals. Students who did not have a major role before might take on one of these roles, or one student might play two roles as the role-play continues.

   Here are the steps students should take in their group work:
   a. List several possible solutions on the Role-Play Solutions Worksheet.
   b. Review each solution and decide if it is realistic.
   c. Choose the best realistic solution.
   d. Practice acting out the solution so they can perform it in front of the class.

5. After the students have practiced their role-plays with solutions, have them perform their role-plays for the rest of the class. If different groups worked on different scenarios, all the solutions for one scenario should be acted out and discussed before moving on to another scenario. It is helpful for students to see several solutions for the same scenario.

6. Remind students of the type of audience behavior you expect before the role-plays are performed.

7. After each role-play, use the questions below to lead a discussion. A key task in the follow-up discussion is to thoroughly evaluate the suggested solutions. Use the following criteria to decide how good each solution would be:
   • Is the solution safe for the people involved? (Solutions should not include using physical force.)

- Is the solution fair? How will the various students involved react to the solution?

- Is the solution practically feasible/realistic (keeping in mind the main characters)?

- Will the solution work, be effective, and lead to the desired result? Why or why not?

- Would this solution work in other situations? Describe situations where it might work and those where it might not work.

These are the basic steps to successfully use role-plays in your class meetings. Once students become comfortable with role-playing, you can branch out to include role-plays on other issues or allow students to come up with their own role-play topics. For a written assignment, you might ask students (individually or in groups) to create a short "play" that could then be performed in class.

·   ·   ·

Dealing with Bullying
on the Individual Level

WHAT YOU WILL LEARN IN CHAPTER 8	• how to intervene on the spot in bullying situations • strategies to talk with students who bully and students who are bullied • how to approach parents of students who bully and students who are bullied • what to do if you suspect bullying might be going on and need to investigate further

It is very important that you take action as soon as you suspect or have been informed of a bullying problem in your classroom. Unfortunately, adults don't always intervene. Sometimes it is because they have trouble recognizing bullying. Some adults don't intervene because they don't see bullying as an important issue. Finally, some adults don't intervene because they are not sure what to do.

In this chapter you will learn how to intervene in a variety of situations and how to talk to parents as well as the students who are directly involved in a bullying situation. You will also learn to deal with different responses from students and parents. You are advised to practice these responses through role-playing with your staff discussion group.

What Should You Do When You See Bullying Happening?

Let's start with situations where you observe bullying happening or need to break up a bullying incident on the spot. You should take the following steps to intervene:

Step 1: Stop the bullying.

Step 2: Support the student who has been bullied.

Duplicating this page is illegal. Do not duplicate without publisher's written permission.

87

Step 3: To the bullying student(s): Name the bullying behavior and refer to the four anti-bullying rules.

Step 4: Empower the bystanders with appreciation if they were supportive to the student who was bullied or with information about how to act in the future.

Step 5: Impose immediate and appropriate consequences for the student(s) who bullied.

Step 6: Take steps to make sure the bullied student will be protected from future bullying.

21

Note: A reproducible tip sheet with these six steps is provided on the Teacher Guide CD-ROM. Make a copy, laminate it, and carry it with you for easy reference.

Here is a more detailed description of the steps outlined above:

STEP	DO's	DONT's
Step 1: Stop the bullying.	Stand between the students who bullied and the student who was bullied. Set ground rules for all participants (for example, "I want you each to stand here and listen and not talk").	Don't get into a verbal or physical tussle with any student. Don't send any students away—especially bystander(s). Don't ask about or discuss the reason for the bullying or try to sort out the facts now.
Step 2: Support the student who has been bullied in a way that allows him or her to regain control of his or her emotions and to "save face."	Stand close beside the student who has been bullied. Make minimal eye contact—just enough to gauge his or her emotions. Consider physically comforting the student (for example, pat the student on the shoulder) only if you think it will not cause him or her to lose control or feel more embarrassed.	Be careful in showing too much overt attention to the student who was bullied. Too much sympathy (when expressed in public) may be uncomfortable for the student. Don't ask the bullied student to tell you what happened. Don't offer lots of sympathy (words or actions) on the spot—wait until later.
Step 3: Address the student(s) who bullied by naming the bullying behavior and refer to the four anti-bullying rules.	State what you saw/heard; label it bullying. State that it is against the school rules (for example, "The words I heard you use are against our rules about bullying").	Do not accuse—simply state the facts ("I saw …" or "I heard …"). Don't engage students in a discussion or argument about the facts. Remind them to listen and not talk.

STEPS continued on next page

STEP	DO's	DONT's
Step 3: continued	Use a matter-of-fact tone to let the student(s) who bullied know exactly what behaviors are not okay and why.	
Step 4: Empower bystanders with appreciation or information about how to act in the future.	Praise bystanders with specific comments about things they did to help, even if they were not effective. If they took no helpful action, use a calm, matter-of-fact, supportive tone to let bystanders know that you noticed their inaction. If appropriate, suggest something they could do now to help the student who was bullied (for example, help to pick up books, accompany him or her to get a new lunch).	Don't scold bystanders for not getting involved. Don't ask bystanders to state what happened or explain their behavior at this point.
Step 5: Impose immediate and appropriate consequences for the student(s) who bullied.	A verbal reprimand is likely to be the first reaction; in addition, you may want to take away some social opportunities from the bullying students as your role and relationship with them permit (for example, recess, lunch in the cafeteria). Let the students who bullied know you will be watching them and their cohorts closely to be sure there is no retaliation against the student who has been bullied. If these students are not members of your classroom, notify their primary teacher so he or she knows what happened and what disciplinarian action was taken (verbal or written). If the students are in middle school/junior high school, notify the teacher who has the closest relationship to the students or your school's discipline officer.	Do not scold. Do not institute a reparation plan on the spot. Follow up later.

STEPS continued on next page

STEP	DO's	DONT's
Step 5: continued	Depending on the system adopted by your school, you may also have to report the incident to your Bullying Prevention Coordinating Committee and/or enter it into a special log.	
Step 6: Take steps to make sure the student who was bullied will be protected from future bullying.	Plan a follow-up meeting with the student who was bullied and his or her parents (as appropriate). Keep an eye on the situation and make sure the student who was bullied knows he or she should report any future bullying to you immediately. Try to involve the student with a positive peer group, so he or she is not isolated or alone.	

Your first reaction when dealing with the bullying students will probably be a verbal rebuke or reprimand. To make a verbal rebuke as effective as possible, keep in mind the following suggestions:

- Intervene as early as possible. It is more difficult to stop a behavior that has "gone too far."

- Approach the students who will be rebuked. Teachers often reprimand students from too far away. If your personal safety is not in danger, then you should be one or two arm lengths away from the students.

- Look the students in the eyes. Tell them to look you in the eyes, if this is culturally appropriate.

- Be brief, clear, and behavior specific. Being specific makes it easier for the students to comply with your request to stop doing what they are doing. For example, saying, "John, you are saying mean things to Emma again. Stop it right now!" is more direct than saying, "Are you making trouble again today, John? How many times have I told you that you have to stop being mean and making trouble?"

- Be firm and determined, but not overly emotional. Your request to stop the behavior should be said in a firm, steady voice with a clear expectation of being obeyed. It is important that you make the student(s) know this is a serious issue without getting too upset or losing control by shouting or making derogatory comments about the students.

- Do not make "empty threats." If the students do not obey you and stop the behavior, be prepared to tell them what negative consequences will occur if they don't stop immediately. Think about what kind of consequences you would apply and make sure you can follow through on them, if necessary.

- Do not tell the students they will have a negative consequence that you are not willing to give. It is important that the students trust that you will do what you say.

- If the students involved are not in your classroom or homeroom, follow up with their classroom or homeroom teachers (or the teacher who has the closest relationship to the students) and possibly the staff member responsible for handling discipline issues at your school, so they are aware of the situation and can help enforce the consequences.

What Type of Consequences Should You Choose?

Several types of consequences were described in chapter 5. You may have freedom to come up with your own consequences for bullying behavior, or your school may have guidelines to follow. Check with your Bullying Prevention Coordinating Committee to verify which approach your school has chosen to take. Following up with consequences will reinforce the message that bullying is not allowed anywhere in the school.

What Type of Follow-Up Should You Do after the Immediate Intervention?

After your initial intervention in a bullying incident, you will need to report the bullying to the students' primary teacher(s) (if you are not yourself the primary teacher) or the staff member who has the closest relationship to each student, and possibly to your school administrators. Consult with your Bullying Prevention Coordinating Committee to be sure you are following your school's plan for reporting bullying incidents.

In many cases, follow-up discussions will be required with the students involved in the bullying incident. You will want to have separate follow-up meetings with the student who was bullied and with the student(s) who bullied. Just note that not all teachers do these kinds of follow-up meetings with students. In some schools, administrators or counselors do this work. Where possible, it is recommended that this follow-up meeting be done by the primary teacher or staff person who has the most positive relationship with each student.

Not every bullying incident will require a follow-up meeting. The extent or severity of the bullying and the likely impact it is having on the bullied student should be considered when deciding whether a follow-up meeting is called for. The amount of reliable information you have about the incident and the bullying relationships between the students involved is another important factor. When in doubt, err on the side of holding meetings. This follow-up meeting should be done as soon after the bullying incident as possible (ideally later that day).

A meeting outline and script for follow-up meetings with both the student who is bullied and the student(s) who bully are discussed later in this chapter.

What Should You Do When You Are Told about a Possible Bullying Problem Involving One of Your Students?

Sometimes you may become aware of a possible bullying problem in your classroom through your class meeting discussions or through reports from classmates of a bullied student, perhaps after a class meeting. Or perhaps the bullied student has contacted you about his or her difficult situation.

If you feel uncertain about the accuracy of the reports received, there are several strategies you can use to find out more information (discussed later in this chapter). As a general guideline, always take reports of bullying very seriously and assume that they are largely correct.

The first step in making sure the information is accurate is to meet with the student who has been reported to be bullied and his or her parents. You may choose to meet first with the student only and then with the parents, or you may schedule a meeting with both the student and parents together.

◆

The one thing I like best about *OBPP* is that it teaches school staff to really concentrate on the student who was bullied first and then deal with the students who are bullying.

— PREVENTION SPECIALIST

Talking with the Student Who Is Being Bullied

A conversation with the student who has been bullied should take place in a quiet room away from the other students. It is best that the rest of the class not know about this meeting. The student may be nervous or anxious about this conversation, so it is important that you let him or her know the purpose of the meeting from the very beginning. An outline and script for this meeting is provided on the Teacher Guide CD-ROM.

For example, you could say, "I am aware that some students in the class have been unkind to you. I'm very sorry this has happened, and now I want to find out a little more about who they are and what has been happening. Then we can talk about how to stop this bullying."

As you continue this discussion, keep in mind the four main objectives to this conversation:

1. To find out as much as possible about what has been happening, who has been doing the bullying, and where and when it has happened. Your conversation with the parents might provide some additional information in this regard.

2. To support the student and to assure him or her that you and other school staff will do everything you can to see that the bullying is stopped.

3. To tell the student that you're sorry that he or she was bullied and that nobody should be treated this way. Explain to the student that you will work together with him or her (and probably his or her parents) to do whatever it takes to stop the bullying. Let the student know that you and the other adults in the school are willing and able to give the student the help he or she needs.

   Ask the student how he or she has been feeling or thinking. This might be a very emotional conversation for the student since he or she has been through some very upsetting experiences. It's important that you allow the student to express his or her emotions, since he or she has probably fought hard to keep them inside. Praise the student for having the courage to discuss these things with you.

4. To inform the student about what action you will take to solve the problem. Let the student know as much as you can about what steps you plan to take to stop the bullying. Tell the student that you intend to talk to the students who have been bullying him or her and make it very clear that the bullying

must stop immediately. Let the student know that you will closely monitor the situation until the bullying has been stopped. Also tell him or her that you will check in with him or her in two or three days to see how things are going.

When you tell the student that you will be talking to the students who bullied, he or she may be worried that the bullying students will try to retaliate for being found out. It is important that you inform the bullying students that you were told about their actions from a variety of different sources (other teachers, several students in the class, and so on). Let the bullied student know that this is what you will tell the bullying students, so that he or she may be less worried about retaliation. Make an agreement with the student to tell the teacher immediately if a new bullying incident occurs. Remind the student that this is not "tattling," but following your school and classroom anti-bullying rules (rule 4). You will also need to talk to the student's parents about this.

Strategies for Contacting and Talking with Parents of a Student Who Is Being Bullied

Note: The term "parents" is used in this chapter, but it refers to parents, guardians, or other family caregivers who have primary responsibility for the well-being of the student involved.

Check with your Bullying Prevention Coordinating Committee to find out who at your school is responsible for contacting parents to talk about bullying that their child may be experiencing (or participating in). In some schools, classroom teachers take on this task. In other schools, the school counselor or principal typically makes these contacts. In still other schools, students who have bullied others are required to call their parents (under the guidance of an adult) to initiate a discussion about their behavior.

Whenever possible, we encourage the classroom teacher or the teacher who has the closest relationship to the student to make this call, owing to the personal relationship they will have with the parents. The person making the calls should have good rapport with the parents and have the patience to work through difficult, emotional situations with them. Your school's administrators and the Bullying Prevention Coordinating Committee will be responsible for creating your school's procedural guidelines on this issue.

Here are some useful guidelines on calling parents about a situation at school where their child is being bullied:

1. If the parents are not available, do not leave details of the bullying situation on a telephone answering machine. Identify yourself and ask them to return your call regarding their son or daughter.

2. If a parent answers the phone, identify yourself and ask if this is a convenient time to talk about a situation regarding their son or daughter. If it is not a good time to talk, ask when you should call back.

3. You may want to start the conversation by saying something like: "It has recently come to my/our knowledge that your son/daughter probably is being bullied by some of his/her classmates (some students at school)."

4. Briefly summarize the situation and ask the parent if he or she would like to continue the discussion by phone or would rather come to the school for a personal meeting.

5. Whatever choice is made, you may follow some or all of the talking points listed below:

   • Report the information you have regarding the situation and ask the parents to tell you what they know about the child's experiences. Answer any questions the parents may have. Depending on the circumstances or your school's policies, you may need to protect the privacy of students and parents involved in bullying by not sharing their names with others. Check with your school's BPCC for guidance on this issue.

   • Invite the parents to work with you and the school to stop the bullying. Explain that they are important partners in this process.

   • Say you're very sorry for the bullying their child has experienced, and assure them that you and your school will do everything possible to get the bullying stopped. Empathize with the parents and their child. Ask the parents if they have advice or suggestions about possible solutions.

   • To the extent that you are able, explain the next steps that will be taken with the bullying students and the consequences for their actions.

   • Ask the parents not to contact the parents of the bullying students, as this may aggravate the situation.

   • Ask the student's parents to report any subsequent acts of bullying or retaliation so that you can take appropriate action.

- Talk to the parents about the student's potential need for counseling and/or additional referral.

- Explain that you're going to check in with their child at school in two to three days and at regular intervals thereafter to see how things are going and that you welcome calls from them at any time. If appropriate, give the parents your direct phone number or email address to make it more convenient for them to call.

- Thank the parents for talking with you.

- Call or meet with the parents later to follow up and inquire how their child is doing. Depending on the situation, this typically should happen within a week. Encourage the parents to keep talking with their child about the situation. Ask about any questions or further concerns. Assure the parents again that they are welcome to call at any time.

A parent tip sheet on working with a child who has been bullied is available (in both English and Spanish) on the Teacher Guide CD-ROM. Share this with the parents as well.

Strategies for Working with Parents Who Call You to Report Bullying Behavior

If it is the parents who contact you with suspicions of or knowledge that their child is being bullied, it is particularly important that you are open to what they have to say. Many parents may find it difficult to contact the school for reasons such as the following:

- They don't want others to know that their child is being singled out for bullying and they may fear humiliation.

- They lack confidence in their ability to encourage the school to help their child.

- They don't know that they have the right to be heard.

- They may feel intimidated by school personnel.

- They may be concerned about communication or cultural barriers if English is not their first language.

- They may be apprehensive about how they will be treated at the school—especially if they have bad memories from their own school days.

- They may be afraid that they will make things worse for their child.

- Their child may be pressuring them not to raise the issue with the school out of fear of retaliation.

So when parents suspect that their child is being bullied, this must be taken very seriously. The first step is to thoroughly investigate the situation. Such an investigation will usually involve talks with the parents who contacted the school and their child, with the students suspected of bullying and other students in the class, and, if appropriate, with parents of other students in the class who may have important information to contribute. Additional investigation strategies are mentioned later in this chapter.

If the suspicion is confirmed, a detailed intervention plan must be drawn up of how you and the school, together with the parents, can put an end to the bullying. Although it is important to involve parents in cases of bullying, it is ultimately the school's responsibility to initiate and coordinate the work in dealing with bullying at school and solving bullying problems.

Talking with the Students Who Are Bullying Others

Once you have had a conversation with the student who is being bullied and his or her parents, you will need to directly confront the bullying student or students. You should do this as quickly as possible after having identified the students involved and gleaned the necessary information. A sample outline and script for this meeting are provided on the Teacher Guide CD-ROM.

As mentioned in chapter 2, bullying is usually carried out by a small group of two to three students. However, about a third of bullied students report that they are mainly bullied by a single student. The following discussion assumes a situation involving more than one bullying student.

It is also most common that the students who bully and the student who is bullied are in the same class. If this is not the case, it would be a good idea to involve the teacher of the bullying students in your conversations too.

It may also be useful to have another adult (such as another teacher, counselor, assistant principal, or school resource officer) included in the conversation with the bullying students, especially if one or more of them could be difficult to handle. Having another adult present sends the message that this is a serious situation. One adult should lead the conversation, however.

You should not talk to the bullying students together as a group. Talk to each one individually and right after one another in quick succession so they have little opportunity to share what was discussed. It is likely that one student played a "leader" role in the bullying. You should talk to this student first, if you know who it is.

Duplicating this page is illegal. Do not duplicate without publisher's written permission.

97

When talking with students who have bullied others, it is most important to make the following points clear:

- You have a number of facts about the situation and you know they have been bullying the other student. Stress that these facts came from several different sources, that many different students have reported the bullying.

- The bullying must stop immediately.

- The negative consequences they will receive (if appropriate, and if not already given).

- You and others will be watching closely to make sure the bullying is discontinued. You will check in with the students involved in two or three days as well as on an ongoing basis to see how things are going.

- There will be more serious negative consequences if the bullying does not stop immediately.

The main objective of these conversations is to end the bullying. The message should be very clear: "We do not accept bullying in our class/school and we will see to it that it comes to an end."

You might begin your conversation by saying something like: "I/we know from a number of sources that there are some students (in the class) that have been mean to or bullied _____ (name of student) lately. We know that you are one of these students. As you know, we do not accept bullying in our class/school and we will see to it that the bullying stops. Is there anything you want to say at this point?"

Also ask for input from the bullying student: "What can you do to improve the situation?" You may also add: "We don't expect you to become good friends with _____, but you must definitely stop treating him or her that way."

Many students who bully are fairly tough and self-assured, and they are good at talking their way out of difficult situations. Here are some common strategies that may be used by students who bully:

Denial

A student who bullies may deny any involvement in the situation. This is why some documentation will be important, so you can state specific details of what happened. Once the student hears this information he or she will realize that you are well informed and may stop denying his or her involvement.

Stress that the information you have about the bullying incident and the student's participation has come from several different sources—that there are many others who have reported that he or she has been involved in the bullying.

Minimizing Their Involvement

Students who bully may also try to trivialize their participation while, at the same time, exaggerating the role of others. They might say, "I'm not the only one who has bullied _____ (name of student)." Your reply could be, "I am aware of that, but now we are talking about your behavior. We will talk to the others later."

Blaming the Student Who Was Bullied

Another common defense is to try to blame the student who was bullied, to make the bullying seem justifiable. For example, students who bully might say that the student's behavior was stupid, irritating, or aggressive (for example, "He/she was the one who started it"). In most cases you can reject this claim because research shows that the majority of bullied students are nonaggressive and do little to provoke other students. You will also most likely have supporting information from other students.

Chapter 2 discussed the relatively small group of students who were called "provocative victims" or "bully-victims." These students often behave in ways that fellow students may find irritating and provoking. If the student who was bullied is one of these students, you might not be able to deny that his or her behavior was annoying. It must be emphasized, however, that even such behavior does not justify bullying. In fact, bullying these students is only likely to make it harder for them to change their behavior.

If the student who was bullied is of the provocative type, you could reply as follows:

"Yes, I/we know that _____ (name of bullied student) now and then may have issues with his/her behavior, but that does not give you the right to bully him/her. We will see what we can do to help this student change his/her behavior. But, in any event, you must stop bullying him/her. As you know, we don't accept bullying in this school. If you think that _____ 's behavior toward you is unacceptable, then you must come and tell me or another adult, so we can address it properly."

After you have spoken individually to all of the students who have been suspected of bullying, you might want to gather them together and talk to them briefly as a group. Remind them that unless the bullying stops now, there will be more severe consequences, and remind them of the follow-up meeting(s).

How Should You Work with Parents of Students Who Are Bullying Others?

It can be particularly difficult to approach the parents of students who bully others. Often these parents are not ready to hear that their child is causing harm to others. For some, this may be the first time they have received such a message.

They may be more supportive of your efforts if they (and all parents) have previously received information about bullying, your school's rules and consequences for bullying, and the procedures for notifying parents of bullying problems. (See chapter 9 for more information about involving parents as partners in the program.)

Also, parents will probably be more receptive if you have established a positive relationship with them prior to this meeting. Many teachers make a point of establishing positive contacts with parents in the first few weeks of school—for example, by sending notes home or calling parents to point out something positive about their children.

Strategies for Contacting and Talking with Parents of a Student Who Is Bullying Others

Here are some guidelines for contacting parents about their child's bullying behavior:

1. Prior to making contact, carefully consider ways that you can help to reduce parents' natural defensiveness. Also review in detail the known facts about their child's involvement in the situation.

2. If the parents are not available, do not leave details of the problem on a telephone answering machine. Identify yourself and ask them to return your call regarding their son or daughter.

3. If a parent answers the phone, identify yourself and ask if this is a convenient time to talk about a situation regarding his or her child. You may want to say something like: "It has recently come to my/our knowledge that your son/daughter has been involved in bullying (or being mean to) another student." Briefly summarize the situation.

4. If the bullying problem is judged to be serious by you or your school administrator, ask the parent to continue the discussion with you in person. Schedule a time when it would be convenient for the parent(s) to come to the school to meet about the situation. For such a personal meeting, choose a private setting and be sure you will not be interrupted. You can determine if you wish to have the student attend the meeting with the parent.

If the problem can be considered relatively nonserious, the conversation can be conducted on the phone, at least as a first step.

5. Whether you meet with parents in person or over the phone, here are some talking points you may like to follow:

- Explain that you are aware of the bullying problem and their child's involvement in this situation (and others, if known).

- Inform the parents that their child has been asked about his or her involvement in the situation.

- You might say something like: "What your child did is an act of bullying, which is unacceptable behavior here at our school. It is against the school rules and we need to work together to make sure that it comes to a *stop*. We assume that you will want to work with us to help your child to stop this behavior."

- You must be prepared for the possibility that parents of a student who bullies other students may try to deny that their child would do such a thing or will try to minimize their child's involvement. Be sure to have concrete examples of their child's behavior that you can share.

- Explain possible next steps with the student (that is, consequences being imposed, if not already given, and monitoring of his or her behavior.)

- Ask what changes or actions the student and his or her parents believe are needed at this point to get the student to stop bullying the other student.

- You may also want to tell the parents that research shows that students who bully other students are at a clearly increased risk of being involved in other antisocial and rule-breaking behaviors such as vandalism, fighting, and early smoking and substance use. For these reasons, bullying behavior should be taken seriously.

- Support parents by saying that you believe that their son or daughter is capable of doing better and that you expect that he or she will do better. Note that with their help, you are certain that the bullying can be stopped. It is important to let parents know that you are not expecting their child to be friends with the targeted student but that you do expect their son or daughter to stop treating him or her that way.

- Discuss the student's potential need for counseling or additional referral.

Duplicating this page is illegal. Do not duplicate without publisher's written permission.

101

- Explain that you're going to check in with their child in two to three days and on an ongoing basis to make sure the bullying has stopped.

- Invite the parents to call or email to discuss concerns regarding this issue or other issues at any time.

6. In the next couple of days arrange another follow-up meeting with the student who bullied (or separate follow-up meetings with all of the students involved in the bullying) to discuss how things are going. Before that meeting, you should have had a meeting with the student who was bullied and at least talked with his or her parents on the phone.

7. Give another follow-up call to the parents of the students who bullied to let them know of their child's improved behavior (or alternatively to discuss an additional course of action to stop the bullying). The monitoring of the bullying students' behavior should not end until it has been established beyond a doubt that the bullying has stopped (and that, hopefully, the student who was bullied now has one or two friends to be with).

A parent tip sheet on how to work with a child who is bullying others is provided (in both English and Spanish) on the Teacher Guide CD-ROM. Plan to share this tip sheet with parents as needed.

How Should You Work with Parents of Students Who Are Bystanders?

During the informational meeting for parents before the program begins (see chapter 9), describe the role of bystanders in bullying situations. Sometimes students passively accept bullying because they don't understand what is happening. Sometimes students actively encourage bullying, even if others are the direct instigators of the bullying behavior. Parents should understand that bystanders possess a great deal of power to stop bullying situations between peers.

The Teacher Guide CD-ROM includes a tip sheet (in both English and Spanish) for parents who are working with a child who has been a bystander in a bullying situation. Share this tip sheet with parents as needed.

Handouts should never replace personal conversations with parents; rather, they are intended to supplement these discussions.

These are some of the important ways you can involve parents in intervening in bullying situations. The next chapter highlights many other ways to get parents involved in *OBPP*.

What Should You Do When You Suspect Bullying
Is Happening but Are Not Certain?

Perhaps you have noted that a certain student is often alone or isolated from the other students. In addition, maybe you have heard some of the student's classmates making derogatory comments about him or her. Yet, no one—not the student, his or her parents, or any classmates—have reported that this student has been isolated intentionally or bullied in other ways. You would like to know more about what is happening with this student, but how can you find out?

You may want to use one or more of the following approaches to gain more information about such a student and his or her relationships with other students. Be sure to document all the information that you obtain from these efforts.

- Observe. As a first step, intensify your observations of the student you suspect is being bullied. Observe the student in the classroom and in other areas of the school, such as the playground/athletic fields, hallways, and lunchroom.

- Focus on finding out how the student is really doing and how his or her classmates are treating him or her. Of course, you will want to be discreet. Try to place yourself where students will not see or notice you. It is a good idea to jot down your observations so you can remember them.

- Check with colleagues. Talk to other staff, especially playground and/or lunchroom supervisors. Ask whether they have noticed that the student is socially isolated or subjected to any negative or humiliating treatment by other students. Share your concerns with your colleagues and ask them to keep a close eye on the student, letting you know what they observe.

- Take a survey. To find out more about this particular student, you may have to gather information from all of your students about the class. Create a simple survey with questions such as the following:

  1. How do you like being in this class?
  2. What are the friendships in this class like?
  3. Do you think that everyone enjoys being in this class? Why or why not?
  4. How many good friends do you have in the class?
  5. Does everyone have someone to be with?
  6. Is there anyone who is bullied?
  7. If you could choose, whom would you most like to be with during recess?
  8. Is there something you would like to change about your class?

In order to ensure that the students' answers are kept confidential, ask the students to fold the sheets in half before handing them in. Alternatively, ask the students to answer the questions at home and turn them in to you in sealed envelopes on the following day.

Make it clear that this information will be used in order to achieve the best possible social relationships in the class. Make sure the students know that if you report the results in class (for example, in class meetings), this will only be done in general terms and without reference to who has written what.

- Conduct in-person interviews with the survey questions. Even though students are told their answers to a written survey will be kept confidential, some may still be afraid to write what they really think. Also, younger students may not be able to write their answers to these questions. In this case, you could use roughly the same survey questions and hold short, personal interviews with all the students. This, of course, takes more time than the written survey, but is an option to consider if you think you will get more relevant information.

- Conduct selected open-ended interviews. Tell the class that you are interested in finding out more about how the students are feeling about the class and their relationships with their classmates. Explain that you would like to interview all of them, but you will only have time to interview five or six of them.

  If you use this strategy, select the student whom you suspect is being bullied as one of the students to interview. Also include some of the social leaders in the class who are popular and less likely to be involved in bullying. It is best if you do not let the class know in advance which students will be interviewed so that students who tend to bully do not have the opportunity to pressure students about what is really going on in the class.

- Combine a survey with some interviews. You could also have students complete a written survey and then interview some students to follow up on their answers. This would allow you to go into more detail about the relationships between students in the class and any bullying behavior that might be going on. You might also want to give students an opportunity to talk to you more personally by meeting with you before or after school. An additional possibility is to invite the students to call you at school if there are things about the peer relationships in the class they would like to discuss.

- Conduct a sociometric survey. A sociometric survey is designed to measure certain aspects of the social relationships in a group of people. This is an easy way to map social isolation and popularity in the classroom. In a sociometric survey, you ask students to write down the names of three students (or maybe four, depending on the size of the class) whom they would like to work with for a group project or assignment.

  When you have received the nominations, tabulate them in a simple (grid) table with the names of all the students both on top and in a row to the left. The names on the top designate the students as nominators and the names to the left the (same) students as possible recipients of nominations. By tabulating who has been nominated by whom and summing the number of nominations for each student (horizontally), you will get a good impression of who is more or less popular and unpopular.

  The fact that a student is not chosen by any of his or her classmates does not necessarily mean that the student is currently being bullied. It does show, however, that he or she is not very well integrated into the peer group and, accordingly, is at increased risk of becoming the target of bullying.

- Contact the parents. It is a good idea to call the parents if you know a student is being socially isolated and maybe bullied. Since you don't know this for sure, and do not want to alarm the parents, the purpose of the call should not be to bring up your suspicions, but to ask how their child likes being in the class. You could ask what the child says at home about school and his or her classmates, explaining that the students are now working on peer relationships in class. If the parents suspect or have knowledge that their child is being bullied at school, they will probably bring up their concerns at this time.

If you have used one or more of the strategies listed above, you will most likely have enough information to determine whether the student in question is being bullied, and you need to take action in ways described in this chapter.

However, if after careful consideration of the collected information, you (maybe in consultation with a school counselor or another teacher) conclude that there is no evidence that the student is being bullied, then you can consider your investigation finished for the time being. The process was worthwhile, as you probably gained insight into the social relationships among the students that will make it easier for you to uncover any problems that might come up in the future.

Working with parents to intervene in bullying situations is very important. There are a number of other ways that you can partner with parents in implementing *OBPP*. The next chapter will introduce you to these strategies.

. . .

9

Partnering with Parents

WHAT YOU WILL LEARN IN CHAPTER 9	• how to develop stronger partnerships with parents • how to involve parents in your classroom bullying prevention strategies • how to arrange classroom-level parent meetings

Note: As in the last chapter, the term "parents" is used here, but it refers to parents, guardians, or other family caregivers who have primary responsibility for the well-being of the student involved.

In the last chapter you learned how to intervene in bullying situations and to talk individually to both students who bully others and students who are bullied. Part of this intervention included talking with parents. Parent involvement is helpful and may even be essential for the smooth running of many aspects of school life. It is also an important component of *OBPP*.

Note: Please keep in mind that this discussion will be describing ideal parent participation, with an understanding that involving parents is often easier said than done. Because families experience numerous demands on scarce time, nearly all schools struggle with finding optimal ways to reach parents and to maximize their involvement.

What Are the Benefits of Actively Involving Parents in *OBPP?*

Parental involvement and support for this program can result in many benefits. First, parents can reinforce the same anti-bullying messages and social rules about caring for others at home. This provides a consistent message for students in all areas of their lives.

Duplicating this page is illegal. Do not duplicate without publisher's written permission.

107

Actively involving parents in positive aspects of the program also improves the likelihood of collaboration and cooperation when bullying situations occur. By informing parents and establishing a positive relationship, some of the uncomfortable aspects of addressing difficult bullying situations can be reduced.

Actively involving parents can also open the door to getting their help in refining and implementing the program in your classroom.

What Are Some of the Issues in Involving Parents in the Classroom?

In a large-scale survey regarding potential measures to prevent and solve school behavior and discipline problems, more than 88 percent of the approximately 3,600 participating teachers answered that "strengthening contact and cooperation with parents" was "very important."[1] Out of a total of twenty-five desirable goals, this was the one that received the greatest support.

Yet there are many reasons why parent participation does not occur as often as it should. Individual teachers, who have rarely received much training in working with parents, may feel uncertain and at a loss. Or they may have had disappointing experiences in the past with parents whom they perceive as "difficult."

Some parents may have had negative school experiences themselves that have left them feeling distrustful, powerless, or worthless in their contact with the school environment. Some may have been bullied themselves. If their child gets into trouble at school, they may feel that school personnel are judging them as parents. Such reactions are not a good starting point for trustful and constructive cooperation with the school.

A positive, cooperative relationship with parents does not happen automatically. A great deal of thought and planning is needed on the part of the teacher and the school to achieve such a result.

Here are some basic guidelines for forming good relationships with parents:

1. Create a positive relationship with parents *before* any problems arise.

2. Start with the assumption that most parents care about their children and want them to be happy and successful in school. Treat parents with respect and believe that they want to be supportive.

3. When a problem does arise, assume a solution-oriented attitude as much as possible. Present the issue as a problem that must be solved and that you, as the teacher, need the parents' help to solve it. Avoid blaming or criticizing the child or the parents. Just state the facts.

How Can You Involve Parents in Your Classroom's Implementation of *OBPP?*

You have probably discovered what types of events or methods are most effective in involving parents in your classroom, given your school population. In your efforts to engage parents in your bullying prevention efforts, consider what works and doesn't work for the parents at your school. Here are some issues to consider:

- time of day/work schedules

- transportation needs

- child care needs

- literacy

- languages spoken

- what attracts parents to school events (personal invitations, student invitations, providing practical information for parents, food, student participation or performances, transportation provided, fun activities, opportunities to talk to the teacher, door prizes, and so on)

This said, even with efforts made on all these fronts, it can be a challenge to involve parents at school. This is particularly true of parents of somewhat older students, in middle or junior high schools, who are typically less inclined to attend school meetings.

Many principals require teachers to call parents during the first few weeks of school to begin establishing a working relationship with them. If you are not required to do so, you will find it well worth the effort. Making an initial positive contact with parents by phone or in person at the beginning of the year lays the groundwork for better communication if you do have to call them about a problem or concern with their child.

Now that your school has decided to implement *OBPP* this is even more important for the following reasons:

- It will be much easier to talk with parents about a bullying problem if you have already established a positive relationship with them.

- Students will be taught to tell an adult if they or someone else is being bullied, and adults (including adults at home) must understand how to react to such information.

- You will have an opportunity to explain the program and how it will work in your school and in your classroom.

- You will have an opportunity to point them to resources and strategies that they can use to help prevent and reduce possible bullying problems.

- You will have an opportunity to encourage parents to talk about bullying with their child at home.
- You will have the opportunity to invite parents to schoolwide and class meetings.

It is important to keep in touch with parents as much as possible. You may already have a home communication system in place, such as a regular newsletter, notes that are sent home, emails, or a Web page. This is a great way to keep parents informed of what is going on in your classroom and to invite them to communicate with you. You can use whatever method you have in place to inform parents of how your class is implementing *OBPP* or other issues.

For more information about talking to parents when a bullying problem occurs, see chapter 8.

Parents can be involved in *OBPP* by:

1. *Supporting the school's Bullying Prevention Coordinating Committee.* It is important that at least one parent serve on this committee to inform and support bullying prevention efforts. Learn who the parent representative on your committee is and offer to help him or her.

2. *Attending classroom parent meetings.* If possible, hold two to three meetings with parents of students in your class over the course of the school year. More information about how to run these meetings is provided later in this chapter.

3. *Helping organize classroom parent meetings.* Ask parents to help organize your classroom parent meetings by offering agenda suggestions, providing food, or calling other parents to remind them to attend.

4. *Attending schoolwide parent meetings.* The kick-off meeting/event will give parents an introduction to *OBPP*, help them understand the need for the program, and identify how they can help at school and at home. Later schoolwide meetings may focus on other relevant topics, including the Olweus Bullying Questionnaire results one year after the initial survey.

   If time permits, combine a schoolwide meeting with discussions in smaller classroom parent meetings. After the small group discussions, all participants reconvene for reporting of viewpoints and a summing-up discussion.

5. *Talking with their children about bullying.* There is a reproducible parent pamphlet about bullying, in both English and Spanish, on the Teacher

Guide CD-ROM that you can mail to parents or send home with your students. This pamphlet provides background information about bullying, suggested strategies for discussing bullying with their children, and an overview of the school's program. This pamphlet also stresses the need for parents to intervene in bullying situations when they become aware of them.

What Should You Do during Classroom-Level Parent Meetings?

Teachers in elementary grades are encouraged to hold classroom-level parent meetings, which are designed to help you and the parents get to know each other better and feel more comfortable with and connected to each other. This improved communication is likely to lead to a more positive class environment. If you work at the middle/junior high school level, consider holding team-level or grade-level meetings instead.

The meetings also provide opportunities for parents to learn more about bullying and related problems, as well as your school's anti-bullying work through *OBPP*. If you don't feel comfortable leading these meetings yourself, ask someone to co-lead the meeting with you, or hold grade-level parent meetings at first.

As mentioned earlier, it is suggested that you hold two to three classroom parent meetings during the school year. These meetings could be held in conjunction with parent-teacher organizational meetings and/or parent conferences. If you teach older students, it might be a good idea to include them in one of these meetings. You may also want to supplement these meetings with one or two social events that include the students, for example, at the end of each semester. These types of events help build a greater sense of community in your classroom.

Room parents or volunteers can help you organize these meetings by

- helping with invitations
- bringing snacks or beverages or asking other parents to do so
- setting up chairs in a circle
- making name tags with both the parent's name and child's name on them
- taking minutes of the meeting and sending them out to all classroom parents

An outline on organizing your first parent meeting is provided on the Teacher Guide CD-ROM. The goal of this first classroom parent meeting will be to introduce the program and the four anti-bullying rules, and to discuss the important role parents can play at home and in support of these efforts at school.

As was mentioned on the previous page, the Teacher Guide CD-ROM includes a reproducible parent pamphlet in both English and Spanish, which can be handed out at a classroom parent meeting.

Here are some possible topics for additional classroom parent meetings:

1. Give parents the opportunity to role-play how to address a situation where their child is being bullied, and then have them role-play how to address a situation where their child is a bystander.

2. How does the media influence students to bully others, including exclusion of others? Discuss how media violence and attitudes on TV, videos, computer and video games, and in music influence student behavior. Also discuss how advertising, sports, and pressure "to be cool" play a part in student behavior and what parents can do to counteract negative media influences.

3. What kinds of rules are most important to parents at home and at school? Give parents the opportunity to share family rules and how they enforce them. They can discuss how these carry over into the child's life at school; for example, bedtimes and curfews, or expectations about how and when homework is to be completed.

4. What were the parents' experiences with bullying when they grew up? Parents can discuss their own experiences with and observations of bullying problems from their youth, how well or poorly these problems were dealt with, how the problems have changed or remained the same, and what lessons can be learned from these experiences.

5. Give updates on how *OBPP* is going in your school and the impact it is having on students, staff, and the school climate.

6. Provide an opportunity for parents to review other parent resources that you have collected that are consistent with *OBPP* (such as videos and books).

What Are Some Additional Tips for Leading Classroom Parent Meetings?

1. Have parents run (or co-lead) these meetings whenever possible as this allows you to participate on the same level as the parents. This may not always be possible, and for some topics (such as the first meeting and the role-playing) it may seem more natural for you to conduct the meeting.

2. Keep the tone friendly and informal, but try to stick to your schedule and meeting topic. One goal of these meetings is to make parents feel more

comfortable coming to you with any bullying problems (or other school-related problems) that are concerning them.

3. If possible, divide the parents into different small groups at each gathering so they have the opportunity to get to know as many parents as possible over the course of the year. If you have established cooperative groups in your classroom, you could use these same groupings for parents at one of the meetings. You and any room parents or volunteers should be divided among the different groups.

4. As a general rule, do not discuss specific bullying problems that may exist in your classroom. The goal of the meetings is to increase parents' general awareness, knowledge, and ability to act in relation to bullying problems. There should be no mention of any bullied or bullying students by name.

   State this at the beginning of the meeting and also in the invitation so that all parents, even those of students who have been bullied or who bully others, will feel comfortable attending the meeting. Only talk about specific bullying situations if the parents of the student who was bullied *and* the students who were bullying give permission to do so.

   This discussion about a specific bullying incident will take skillful leadership on your part. You may want to invite another teacher or a member of the Bullying Prevention Coordinating Committee to participate in such a meeting. Another, safer strategy to deal with an identified bullying problem would be to follow the procedures outlined in chapter 8.

5. Have a general discussion about the relationships among the students and the social climate of the classroom. This will help parents understand what their children experience day to day.

6. Invite parents who want to talk about their child's situation to call you, email you, or set up a time to meet with you in person.

7. Vary the topics of parent meetings, so parents do not lose interest. For example, including role-plays or discussions about media influences or family rules in addition to bullying might help to keep parents motivated to attend.

Going Beyond the Basic Program

WHAT YOU WILL LEARN IN CHAPTER 10	• what program components you should continue to do over the long term • additional ways to enhance *OBPP* • how to select appropriate bullying prevention resources to supplement your *OBPP* efforts

As mentioned earlier, *OBPP* is not a curriculum with a prescribed number of sessions. Instead, it is designed to become a component of the school environment and part of your classroom routine. To be successful, the program needs to be continued for more than just a year or two. Research has shown that using the program over the long term produces continued success in reducing bullying and other antisocial behavior.

It is also important to be aware that bullying is a problem that will not be completely erased even with your best efforts. Bullying tendencies can arise at any time, and you must be constantly prepared to prevent and actively counter this type of problem. This is partly due to the nature of bullying behavior and partly due to the fact that individual school populations are constantly changing (students move away or move on to other schools). It is therefore necessary to repeat certain components of *OBPP* regularly.

Continue the Core Program over the Long Term

One of the main ways you can continue the program in your classroom is to maintain your weekly class meetings. You will find these meetings to be beneficial in many ways, including building a sense of community and caring in your classroom. These class meetings should be used to update and maintain the anti-bullying rules and to keep up the students' commitment and understanding of your school's bullying policies.

You should also continue to use role-playing as much as possible. Although bullying will be a main theme in class meetings, it is natural that they will gradually also focus on other topics related to the students' behavior, their well-being, and the school environment.

Your consistent use of positive and negative consequences should also become part of your classroom routine. Students will depend on your fair and consistent use of consequences throughout the school year. Once they see adults intervening in bullying situations, they will also rely on adults to take action when needed. It takes time and consistency to build up these expectations, but they will then become key components in preventing bullying in your classroom.

Also be sure to continue meeting and talking with your students' parents, and continue to meet regularly with other teachers in your staff discussion groups. You can gain new ideas or insights by listening to the experiences of others. Also plan to attend any booster trainings that your Bullying Prevention Coordinating Committee may provide.

You will also be asked to administer the Olweus Bullying Questionnaire on a yearly basis. This ongoing assessment is helpful in determining ways to improve your program over the long term.

Integrate Bullying Topics into Your Curriculum

You can expand your anti-bullying efforts in the classroom by integrating the topic into your curriculum as much as possible. As time goes on you might find that certain issues around bullying need more time and attention. You may want to find ways to address these issues through the curriculum you teach.

For example, perhaps you would like to focus more on how bystanders react to bullying situations. This would be a good time to include a supplemental activity that also meets your academic goals, such as writing stories, plays, or creating videos that demonstrate how bystanders can take an active role in stopping bullying.

In a unit on media literacy, for example, you could have students use different types of advertising techniques to get an anti-bullying message across to bystanders in your school. Perhaps your students could watch a film that contains a student who bullies and at least one bystander and write a film review or character sketch. Be creative. There are many ways to address bullying that can also help you meet the academic standards for your class. Here is one example:

In Lynn, Massachusetts, middle school students videotaped interviews with fellow students, asking about their experiences with bullying, how it made them feel, and what they thought could be done to stop bullying. Students edited and produced the video and presented it during a parent kick-off event.

Students may be more likely to retain messages instilled by *OBPP* when they are able to relate them to their own lives and experiences. Linking *OBPP* concepts to academic themes reinforces concepts and helps students make connections to their own lives.

Anti-bullying themes can be linked with the academic curriculum in a variety of ways based on the developmental level of your students. There are natural links to language arts, social studies and history, health/psychology, art/music/drama, and even math, science, physical education, and foreign languages. Suggestions for integrating bullying topics into different school subjects are provided on the Teacher Guide CD-ROM.

As part of your bullying prevention efforts, you may also want to look for opportunities to build community—for example, by cross-class or cross-grade activities. Such opportunities help students get to know others outside of their individual classrooms, assume different roles in group cooperative work, and so on.

Selecting Appropriate Bullying Prevention Resources

You might want to look for other resources such as books, videos, or CD-ROMs on bullying and related topics. Information on annotated bibliographies of bullying resources is provided on the Teacher Guide CD-ROM.

Here are some tips for selecting appropriate bullying prevention resources:

1. Be sure that the books, videos, and other resources selected for children and youth are developmentally appropriate. A description of the intended age group is usually provided. If not, review the abstract or story line and consider the ages of the main characters.

2. Look for materials that are ethnically and culturally diverse and that avoid stereotypes.

3. Look for materials that explain and illustrate the many forms that bullying can take, such as physical and verbal bullying, social exclusion, and cyber-bullying.

4. Select materials that show both boys *and* girls involved in bullying and present opportunities for discussions about gender issues in bullying.

5. Look for materials that suggest or show appropriate and realistic solutions to bullying problems. Look for stories that depict adults as positive role models, who are capable of dealing with bullying without humiliating the students who bully or embarrassing or blaming students who are bullied.

6. Find stories that show appropriate ways for students and adults to stop bullying when they see it and offer support to those who are bullied. Avoid resources that suggest that bullying can easily be dealt with alone or without support from others.

Warning Signs of Questionable Resources

Beware of resources that inaccurately "stereotype" students who bully or students who are bullied. For example, use caution with resources that show

- Students who bully are always boys.
- Students who bully are always unpopular misfits.
- Students who are bullied always look "different" from other students—they are always overweight, disabled, or wear funny clothes. Bullying can happen to anyone.

Beware of resources that portray simplistic, unrealistic, or harmful solutions to bullying, such as where

- A student who bullies others is publicly humiliated or injured.
- A student who is bullied physically retaliates against the students who bully him or her.
- Peer mediation or conflict resolution strategies are used to resolve bullying.
- A student who is bullied becomes good friends with his or her tormentor. (Although this can happen, it usually isn't realistic to expect these students to become good friends.)
- A simple "one size fits all" approach is recommended.

Beware of resources that downplay or minimize the effects of bullying on students. Bullying is a very serious issue and should not be dealt with lightly. Bullying can be extremely harmful to students who are bullied and is often a sign of other serious antisocial and/or violent behavior.

If you have questions about resources or how to integrate bullying topics into your curriculum, contact your Bullying Prevention Coordinating Committee or your school's certified Olweus trainer.

A list of Web sites that have recommended resources can also be found on your Teacher Guide CD-ROM.

Getting Students Involved in Community Efforts

It is a great learning experience for students to see what impact they can make on bullying within their community. The Teacher Guide CD-ROM includes a list of activities you could do with older students around community efforts.

Thank you for your commitment to making a difference in your students' lives. We hope this guide provides you with the basic steps needed to implement *OBPP* successfully in your classroom. Not only will you be changing the climate of your classroom, you will be impacting the quality of your students' lives both now and in the future.

Duplicating this page is illegal. Do not duplicate without publisher's written permission.

119

Notes

Chapter 1: Introducing the *Olweus Bullying Prevention Program*

1. Dan Olweus, "Bully/Victim Problems among Schoolchildren: Basic Facts and Effects of a School-Based Intervention Program," in *The Development and Treatment of Childhood Aggression,* ed. D. Pepler and K. Rubin (Hillsdale, N.J.: Erlbaum, 1991), 411–48; Dan Olweus, "A Useful Evaluation Design, and Effects of the Olweus Bullying Prevention Program," *Psychology, Crime & Law* 11 (2005): 389–402; Dan Olweus and S. Limber, *Blueprints for Violence Prevention: Bullying Prevention Program* (Boulder: Program Institute of Behavioral Science, University of Colorado, 1999); Jan Helge Kallestad and Dan Olweus, "Predicting Teachers' and Schools' Implementation of the Olweus Bullying Prevention Program: A Multilevel Study," *Prevention and Treatment* 6 (October 2003): 3–21. Available on the Internet: http://www.journals.apa.org/prevention/ volume6/pre0060021a.html.

2. Kallestad and Olweus, "Predicting Teachers' and Schools' Implementation of the Olweus Bullying Prevention Program."

3. Dan Olweus, "Bully/Victim Problems among Schoolchildren: Basic Facts and Effects of a School-Based Intervention Program," in *The Development and Treatment of Childhood Aggression*, ed. D. Pepler and K. Rubin (Hillsdale, N.J.: Erlbaum, 1991), 411–48.

4. Dan Olweus, "Vad Skapar Aggressiva Barn?" [What Creates Aggressive Children?] in *Normkrise og Oppdragelse* [Norm Crisis and Child Rearing], ed. A. O. Telhaug and S. E. Vestre (Oslo, Norway: Didakta, 1981); Dan Olweus, "Sweden," in *The Nature of School Bullying: A Cross-National Perspective,* ed. P. K. Smith, Y. Morita, J. Junger-Tas, D. Olweus, R. Catalano, and P. Slee (London: Routledge, 1999), 7–27.

Chapter 2: Recognizing the Many Faces of Bullying

1. Dan Olweus, *Bullying at School: What We Know and What We Can Do* (Oxford, England: Blackwell Publishing, 1993).

2. P. K. Smith, "Play Fighting and Real Fighting: How Do They Relate?" (paper presented at ICCP Conference in Lisbon, Portugal, October 1997).

3. Olweus, *Bullying at School.*

4. Dan Olweus, *Mobbing i skolen: Nye data om omfang og forandring over tid* [Bullying at School: New Data on Prevalence and Change Over Time] (Bergen, Norway: Research Center for Health Promotion, University of Bergen, 2002).

5. G. B. Melton, S. P. Limber, P. Cunningham, D. W. Osgood, J. Chambers, V. Flerx, and others, Violence among Rural Youth: Final Report (Washington, D. C.: U.S. Department of Justice, Office of Justice Programs, Office of Juvenile Justice and Delinquency Prevention, 1998).

6. T. Nansel and others, "Bullying Behaviors among U.S. Youth," *Journal of the American Medical Association* 285, no. 16 (2001): 2094–2100.

7. All of the studies mentioned here have used the global questions from the Olweus Bullying Questionnaire (original or revised version) from: Dan Olweus, *The Revised Olweus Bully/Victim Questionnaire* (Bergen, Norway: Research Center for Health Promotion, University of Bergen, 1996); and M. Solberg and Dan Olweus, "Prevalence Estimation of School Bullying with the Olweus Bully/Victim Questionnaire," *Aggressive Behavior* 29 (2003): 239–68.

8. Dan Olweus, *Bullying at School;* M. Solberg, D. Olweus, and I. Endresen, "Bullies and Victims at School: Are They the Same Pupils?" *British Journal of Education Research* (in press); P. K. Smith, K. C. Madsen, and J. C. Moody, "What Causes the Age Decline in Reports of Being Bullied at School? Towards a Developmental Analysis of Risks of Being Bullied," *Educational Research* 41 (1999): 267–85.

9. E. E. Maccoby, "Social Groupings in Childhood: Their Relationships to Prosocial and Antisocial Behavior in Boys and Girls," in *Development of Antisocial and Prosocial Behavior*, ed. D. Olweus, J. Block, and M. Radke-Yarrow (New York: Academic Press, 1986).

10. More detailed information on the characteristics of students involved in bullying problems is available in Dan Olweus, *Bullying at School: What We Know and What We Can Do* (Oxford, England: Blackwell Publishing, 1993) 34–39 and 53–60.

11. Solberg, Olweus, and Endresen, "Bullies and Victims at School"; Dan Olweus, *Aggression in the Schools: Bullies and Whipping Boys* (Washington, D.C.: Hemisphere (Wiley), 1978); Olweus, *Bullying at School.*

12. Olweus, *Bullying at School*; F. D. Alsaker and Dan Olweus, "Stability and Change in Global Self-Esteem and Self-Related Affect," in *Understanding the Self of the Early Adolescent*, ed. T. M. Brinthaupt and R. P. Lipka (New York: New York State University of New York Press, 2001).

13. D. S. Hawker and M. J. Boulton, "Twenty Years' Research on Peer Victimization and Psychosocial Maladjustment: A Meta-analytic Review of Cross-Sectional Studies," *Journal of Child Psychology and Psychiatry* 41 (2000) 441–55; J. Juvonen, S. Graham, and M. A. Schuster, "Bullying among Young Adolescents:

The Strong, the Weak, and the Troubled," *Pediatrics* 112 (2003): 1231–37; Olweus, *Bullying at School*; Olweus, *Aggression in the Schools*.

14. Dan Olweus, "Victimization by Peers: Antecedents and Long-Term Outcomes," in *Social Withdrawal, Inhibition and Shyness,* ed. K. H. Rubin and J. B. Asendorf (Hillsdale, N.J.: Lawrence Erlbaum, 1993), 315–41.

15. M. Solberg, D. Olweus, and I. Endresen, *Bullies, Victims, and Bully-Victims: How Deviant Are They and How Different?* (Bergen, Norway: Research Center for Health Promotion, University of Bergen, forthcoming); Dan Olweus, "Peer Harassment. A Critical Analysis and Some Important Issues," in *Peer Harassment in School: The Plight of the Vulnerable and Victimized,* ed. J. Juvonen and S. Graham (New York: Guilford Publications, 2001), 3–20; D. Schwartz, L. J. Proctor, and D. H. Chien, "The Aggressive Victim of Bullying: Emotional and Behavioral Dysregulation as a Pathway to Victimization by Peers," in *Peer Harassment in School: The Plight of the Vulnerable and Victimized,* ed. J. Juvonen and S. Graham (New York: The Guilford Press, 2001).

16. Olweus, *Bullying at School*.

17. P. B. Cunningham, S. W. Henggeler, S. P. Limber, G. B. Melton, and M. A. Nation, "Patterns and Correlates of Gun Ownership among Nonmetropolitan and Rural Middle School Students," *Journal of Clinical Child Psychology* 29 (2000): 432–42.

18. Olweus, *Bullying at School;* Juvonen, Graham, and Schuster, "Bullying among Young Adolescents," 1231–37; R. J. Baumeister, J. D. Campbell, J. I. Krueger, and K. D. Vohs, "Does Self-Esteem Cause Better Performance, Interpersonal Success, Happiness, or Healthier Lifestyles?" *Psychological Science in the Public Interest* 4 (2003): 1–44.

19. Olweus, *Bullying at School*.

20. Dan Olweus, "Familial and Temperamental Determinants of Aggressive Behavior in Adolescent Boys: A Causal Analysis," *Developmental Psychology* 16 (1980): 644–60; Olweus, *Bullying at School*.

21. A. C. Baldry, "Bullying in Schools and Exposure to Domestic Violence," *Child Abuse & Neglect* 27 (2003): 713–32.

22. I. Endresen and Dan Olweus, "Participation in Power Sports and Antisocial Involvement in Preadolescent and Adolescent Boys," *Journal of Child Psychology and Psychiatry* 46 (2005): 468–78; B. J. Bushman and C. A. Anderson, "Media Violence and the American Public: Scientific Facts Versus Media Misinformation," *American Psychologist* 57 (2002), 477–489.

23. C. Salmivalli, K. Lagerspetz, K. Björkqvist, K. Osterman, and A. Kaukiainen, "Bullying as a Group Process: Participant Roles and Their Relations to Social Status within the Group," *Aggressive Behavior* 22 (1996): 1–15.

24. Dan Olweus, "Peer Harassment: A Critical Analysis and Some Important Issues," in *Peer Harassment in School*, ed. J. Juvonen and S. Graham (New York: Guilford Publications, 2001): 3–20.

25. Dan Olweus, "Aggression and Peer Acceptance in Adolescent Boys: Two Short-Term Longitudinal Studies of Ratings," *Child Development* 48 (1977): 1301–13; Dan Olweus, "Stability of Aggressive Reaction Patterns in Males: A Review," *Psychological Bulletin* 86 (1979): 852–75.

26. Dan Olweus, *Hackkycklingar och översittare: Forskning om Skolmobbning* [Whipping Boys and Bullies: Research about School Bullying] (Stockholm: Almqvist & Wiksell, 1973); Olweus, *Aggression in the Schools*.

27. Nansel and others, "Bullying Behaviors among U.S. Youth."

28. Olweus, *Bullying at School*.

29. Ibid.

30. Ibid.

31. T. R. Nansel, M. D. Overpeck, D. L. Haynie, W. J. Ruan, and P. C. Scheidt, "Relationships between Bullying and Violence among U.S. Youth," *Archives of Pediatric Adolescent Medicine* 157 (2003): 348–53; J. D. Unnever and D. G. Cornell, "The Culture of Bullying in Middle School," *Journal of School Violence* 2, vol. 2 (2003): 5–27.

32. Olweus, *Bullying at School;* Juvonen, Graham, and Schuster, "Bullying among Young Adolescents," 1231–37; Baumeister and others, "Does Self-Esteem Cause Better Performance, Interpersonal Success, Happiness, or Healthier Lifestyles?" 1–44.

33. Nansel and others, "Bullying Behaviors among U.S. Youth."

34. Olweus, *Bullying at School*.

35. Ibid.

36. M. Solberg, D. Olweus, and I. Endresen, *Bullies, Victims, and Bully-Victims: How Deviant Are They and How Different?* (Bergen, Norway: Research Center for Health Promotion, University of Bergen, forthcoming).

37. R. Kowalski, S. P. Limber, A. Scheck, M. Redfern, J. Allen, A. Calloway, J. Farris, K. Finnegan, M. Keith, S. Kerr, L. Singer, J. Spearman, L. Tripp, and L. Vernon, "Electronic Bullying among School-Aged Children and Youth" (paper presented at the annual meeting of the American Psychological Association, Washington, D.C., August 2005).

38. National Mental Health Association, "Bullying in Schools: Harassment Puts Gay Youth at Risk" (2002).

39. Harris Interactive, Inc. and GLSEN, *From Teasing to Torment: School Climate in America, A Survey of Students and Teachers* (New York: GLSEN, 2005). This report can be accessed on the Internet at www.glsen.org/binary-data/GLSEN_ATTACHMENTS/file/585-1.pdf.

40. Dan Olweus, *Mobbing av Elever fra Lærere* [Bullying of Students by Teachers] (Bergen, Norway: Alma Mater forlag, 1996); Dan Olweus, "Sweden," in *The Nature of School Bullying: A Cross-National Perspective,* ed. P. K. Smith, Y. Morita, J. Junger-Tas, D. Olweus, R. Catalano, and P. Slee (London: Routledge, 1999), 28–48.

41. S. W. Twemlow, P. Fonagy, F. C. Sacco, and J. R. Brethour, "Teachers Who Bully Students: A Hidden Trauma," *International Journal of Social Psychiatry* 52 (2006): 187–98.

Chapter 3: Supporting Schoolwide Implementation of the Program

1. Dan Olweus, *Bullying at School: What We Know and What We Can Do* (Oxford, England: Blackwell Publishing, 1993), 25.

Chapter 4: Getting Started in the Classroom

1. Dan Olweus and F. D. Alsaker, "Assessing Change in a Cohort Longitudinal Study with Hierarchical Data," in *Problems and Methods in Longitudinal Research,* ed. D. Magnusson, L. R. Bergman, G. Rudinger, and B. Törestad (New York: Cambridge University Press, 1991), 107–32.

Chapter 5: Setting Rules and Creating a Positive Classroom

1. Dan Olweus and F. D. Alsaker, "Assessing Change in a Cohort Longitudinal Study with Hierarchical Data," in *Problems and Methods in Longitudinal Research*, ed. D. Magnusson, L. R. Bergman, G. Rudinger, and B. Törestad (New York: Cambridge University Press, 1991), 107–32.

2. S. P. Limber, "Addressing Youth Bullying Behaviors," in *Educational Forum on Adolescent Health: Youth Bullying*, ed. M. Fleming and K. Towey (Chicago: American Medical Association, 2002), 5–16.

Chapter 6: Holding Class Meetings

1. Dan Olweus and F. D. Alsaker, "Assessing Change in a Cohort Longitudinal Study with Hierarchical Data," in *Problems and Methods in Longitudinal Research,* ed. D. Magnusson, L. R. Bergman, G. Rudinger, and B. Törestad (New York: Cambridge University Press, 1991), 107–32.

Chapter 7: Using Role-Plays

1. Dan Olweus and F. D. Alsaker, "Assessing Change in a Cohort Longitudinal Study with Hierarchical Data," in *Problems and Methods in Longitudinal Research*, ed. D. Magnusson, L. R. Bergman, G. Rudinger, and B. Törestad (New York: Cambridge University Press, 1991), 107–32.

Chapter 9: Partnering with Parents

1. T. Ogden, *Elevatferd og Læringsmilijø* [Student Behavior and the Learning Environment] (Oslo: Ministry of Church, Education, and Research, 1998).

. . .

About the Authors and Contributors

Authors

Dan Olweus, Ph.D.

For more than thirty-five years, Dr. Dan Olweus, research professor of psychology, affiliated with the Research Center for Health Promotion (HEMIL) at the University of Bergen in Norway, has been involved in research and intervention work in the area of bullying problems among schoolchildren and youth. In 1970, he started a large-scale project that is now generally regarded as the first scientific study of bullying problems in the world, published as a book in Scandinavia in 1973 and in 1978 in the United States under the title *Aggression in the Schools: Bullies and Whipping Boys*.

In the 1980s, Dr. Olweus conducted the first systematic intervention study against bullying in the world, which documented a number of quite positive effects of what is now the *Olweus Bullying Prevention Program (OBPP)*. He was also the first to study the problem of bullying of students by teachers. Since 2001, he has been the leader of a government-initiated national initiative implementing *OBPP* on a large-scale basis in Norwegian elementary and junior high schools.

Dr. Olweus is generally recognized as a pioneer and founding father of research on bullying problems and as a world-leading expert in this area both by the research community and by society at large. His book *Bullying at School: What We Know and What We Can Do* has been translated into fifteen different languages. Dr. Olweus has received a number of awards and recognitions for his research and intervention work, including the "Distinguished Contributions to Public Policy for Children" award by the Society for Research in Child Development (SRCD). He has been a fellow at the Center for Advanced Study in the Behavioral Sciences (CASBS) in Stanford, California.

Susan P. Limber, Ph.D., MLS

Susan P. Limber is director of the Center on Youth Participation and Human Rights and professor of psychology at Clemson University. She is a developmental psychologist who received her masters and doctoral degrees in psychology at the University of Nebraska–Lincoln. She also holds a Masters of Legal Studies from Nebraska.

Dr. Limber's research and writing have focused on legal and psychological issues related to youth violence (particularly bullying among children), child protection, and children's rights. She directed the first wide-scale implementation and evaluation of the *Olweus Bullying Prevention Program* in the United States and co-authored the *Blueprint for the Bullying Prevention Program* as well as many other articles on the topic of bullying. In recent years, she has directed the training for the *Olweus Bullying Prevention Program* in the United States. She has provided consultation to the National Bullying Prevention Campaign, supported by the Health Resources and Services Administration.

In 1997, she received the Saleem Shah Award for early career excellence in psychology-law policy, awarded by the American Psychology-Law Society of the American Psychological Association (Division 41) and the American Academy of Forensic Psychiatry. In 2004, Dr. Limber received the American Psychological Association's Early Career Award for Psychology in the Public Interest.

Contributors

Vicki Crocker Flerx, Ph.D.

Vicki C. Flerx is an *Olweus Bullying Prevention Program* training director and a research assistant professor at the University of South Carolina's Institute for Families in Society. She has expertise in both public and mental health. Prior to earning her doctorate in public health, Dr. Flerx spent fifteen years as a therapist working in psychiatric settings and focusing on women and youth who were victims of abuse. Dr. Flerx was one of the University of South Carolina researchers who first brought the *Olweus Bullying Prevention Program* to the United States. Dr. Flerx trains and consults nationally to support the dissemination of the program. In addition, she has conducted research in family violence, including intimate partner violence, child abuse, and children exposed to domestic violence.

Nancy Mullin, M.Ed.

Nancy Mullin is an *Olweus Bullying Prevention Program* training director and a research scientist at the Wellesley Centers for Women at Wellesley College, where she is director of both the Project on Teasing and Bullying and the Preschool Empathy Project. Ms. Mullin is a nationally known trainer and consultant in the area of bullying prevention and developing awareness about the negative effects that bullying and related gender-role stereotypes have on both school climate and student performance. She has been involved in research, curriculum development, and training. She also coordinated the Massachusetts Bullying Prevention Project, the first statewide *Olweus Bullying Prevention Program* school initiative in the United States. Ms. Mullin is the author of several publications about bullying, including *Quit It! A Teacher's Guide on Teasing and Bullying for Use with Students in Grades K–3,* a recommended *OBPP* supplemental resource.

Jane Riese, L.S.W.

Jane Riese is an *Olweus Bullying Prevention Program* training director as well as the director of Bullying Prevention Services at Family-Child Resources, Inc. in York, Pennsylvania. A social worker and prevention educator since 1982, Ms. Riese helped to pilot the early Olweus trainers certification process and assisted with coordination of the first U.S. Olweus Training of Trainers held in 2001 in Pennsylvania. She currently oversees *Olweus Bullying Prevention Program* implementation in numerous schools throughout the country. Ms. Riese created and directed dialogue-based restorative justice programming in her community and was also the director of a prosecution-based victim-witness office. She has served on the board of directors of the international Victim Offender Mediation Association since 2000.

Marlene Snyder, Ph.D.

Marlene Snyder is an associate professor at the Institute of Family and Neighborhood Life, Clemson University, in South Carolina and serves as the *Olweus Bullying Prevention Program's* national point of contact. She can be contacted at nobully@clemson.edu or 1-864-710-4562.

Dr. Snyder is also a training director for the *Olweus Bullying Prevention Program.* She has served as a national and international conference speaker, trainer, and technical assistance consultant for educational, mental health, child welfare, and juvenile justice agencies, as well as parent education organizations. Dr. Snyder consults regularly with a wide variety of professional and community organizations on a range of topics related to bullying prevention and intervention. She has also written extensively on the topic of ADHD, including a book entitled *ADHD & Driving: A Guide for Parents of Teens with ADHD.* Dr. Snyder is the founding president of the International Bullying Prevention Association.